# The
# Derby
# Scene

*DERBY*
# Evening Telegraph

# The Derby Scene

by
Geoff Hammerton

The Breedon Books
Publishing Company
Derby

First published in Great Britain by
The Breedon Books Publishing Company Limited
44 Friar Gate, Derby, DE1 1DA
1993

ISBN 1 873626 55 X

Printed and bound by Hillmans Printers, Frome, Somerset.
Covers printed by BDC Printing Services Limited of Derby.

# *Contents*

This book is dedicated to the photographers of the *Derby Evening Telegraph* who took the great majority of these pictures over the years, particularly Dick Arnold — chief photographer in the 1950s and 1960s — who may be spotted between the ranks in the picture of Derby School Combined Cadet Force on parade in 1954.

# Introduction

NOSTALGIA, some wit once said, is not what it used to be. Of course, he said that a long time ago and it is no longer true . . .! We all like remembering the past, reliving happy memories and finding that even the sad times had their happier moments. We would not want to live back in the past . . .or would we? We remember a more relaxed pace of life in which there was time to do things, difficult though they might be to do. Would we want to lose today's fast-acting hi-tech, with every convenience at the touch of a remote control, in exchange for those often hard times of our youth? The past is surely best when held in memory.

To help you to remember, to evoke the magic of the mind, take a leisurely stroll through these pages of pictures of Derby's past, but not very long past. We are going on a journey through the years and through the streets of Derby, to see the places and faces that used to be, to see how the scene changed and to realise how different many things now are from what they were a mere 20 years ago.

We are covering the 50 years from 1920 to 1970, give or take a few years either side. It is roughly the middle half of our century.

The pictures should have appeal for three groups of readers. First, those who have lived in Derby through all those years, have watched the changes and can now look back remembering them. Second, those who have lived here through some of that time and can mix memories with the discovery of what happened before. And third, those who are finding out for the first time about Derby in those years, either because they are too young to remember or have come to know the city more recently.

I put myself in the middle class. I came to Derby in 1958, so the last quarter of the period is in my memory. Some of the scenes and happenings of the earlier years I had heard about, some experiences, such as the war years, I had similarly undergone in another place. It has been a fascinating exercise to probe and find other new things about the old town. It is a fascination I now want to share with you.

The photographs come from the extensive picture library of the *Derby Evening Telegraph*. Some may be familiar to you, having been used in other places; others are being used for the first time anywhere.

The choices of which to use have been mine and I take responsibility for omissions and for any errors in the captions commentary I have written to go with them. All credit for the pictures goes to the *Telegraph* photographers of the past whose contemporary record of their times now becomes a pictorial history of Derby in the mid-20th century.

My thanks go to the staff of the *Telegraph* picture library for helping in my search for the right photographs and to the staff of the Derby Local Studies Library where I was able to check information in the photographic files of the *Telegraph*. My apologies go to my wife, Carol, for leaving piles of pictures and papers around the house and for so frequently shutting myself away with the word processor; my thanks to her for the encouraging comment, "Well, that's good!" always following my answer to her frequent question about how far I was through the 400 pictures that comprise this scenic Derby journey.

G.D.Hammerton
Mickleover
August 1993

# Royal Occasions

This elegant entrance pavilion was first erected at Osmaston Park for the Royal Show of 1906 and was there for subsequent ones in 1921 and 1933. The 1906 Show was attended by King Edward VII who had previously been to Derby, as Prince of Wales, when the Royal Show was held at Osmaston Park in 1881. The first time Derby provided a venue for the Royal Show was 1843 — it is not clear whether Queen Victoria attended but she and Prince Albert certainly did visit Derby some time that year.

Hats off for the King — but then quickly back on again. The sequence of the men's raising of hats as the grey-toppered George V walks by is captured in this memory of the Royal Show at Osmaston Park in June 1921. The bus in front of which they are standing appears to be one from Salford Corporation, part of a display of transport.

Not exactly a royal walkabout — more a formal inspection. The King chats to a policeman, standing in one of several lines of privileged people meeting, or at least being seen by George V on that 1921 Royal Show visit. The King travelled by train and was in Derby for four hours. The five-day show drew a record attendance of 125,000.

Smiling, waving crowds throng the streets of the town as George V and Queen Mary, parasol raised, drive through Derby on their way to the Royal Show at Osmaston Park in July 1933. This was the record fifth — but last — time the Royal Show was held there. It was also the last visit by George V to Derby; he died in January 1936.

Make way for the royal landau. It seems there is scarcely room to get through the crowds as the King and Queen arrive at the showground.

The Duke of Devonshire — the ninth duke, grandfather of the present 11th — walks alongside Queen Mary as she tours the stands of Derby's trade and commerce.

A couple of months before the 1933 visit by the King and Queen, their son, the Duke of York, later King George VI, was in town for a little less formal occasion. He was received by the directors and toured the Derby works of Ley's Malleable Castings — with workmen in the background taking as much interest in him as he took in the foundry processes.

It was bowler hats all round — well, almost — as on the same occasion the Duke went out of town to see more of the area's heavy industry at Stanton Ironworks.

The King is dead. And patiently, on Sunday, 26 January 1936, the people of Derby slowly wind their way in a long queue through the town centre to see the wreath being sent by Derby for the funeral of George V at Windsor.

Their long wait in the queue is over. They have reached the Guildhall foyer where the wreath, in the form of an anchor, was on display throughout the Sunday, two days before the funeral at Windsor.

Long live the King. It is 12 May 1937 and, as in the rest of the country and the empire, Derby was celebrating the Coronation of George VI. The guns of the Derby TA Field Battery of the Royal Artillery boom out a royal salute in Siddals Fields.

Coronation Day duties for Councillor Mrs Elizabeth Petty, Derby's first woman Mayor, included a tree-planting but here she turns to a quite different 12 May duty — laying a wreath at the statue of Florence Nightingale near Derbyshire Royal Infirmary in London Road, to mark the 117th anniversary of the birth of this Lady with the Lamp.

Everywhere there are street parties, paper hats, flags, tables and goodies brought out into the decorated streets. Here are Coronation Day scenes in Dale Road and Stanhope Street.

More Coronation Day street parties in Thrupps's Yard off Harrington Street and Norman Street.

The visitors are the Gloucesters. The Duke of Gloucester, the King's brother, is in the uniform of an Air Marshal for a wartime visit, in February 1943, that included an inspection of the underground ammunition dump at RAF Fauld where, less than two years later, the devastating explosion occurred, the world's biggest pre-atomic explosion.

Nearly 20 years separated two visits by the Duchess of Gloucester (above and opposite). In October 1936 she is in Derby to lay the foundation stone of extensions to Derbyshire Royal Infirmary. With her are Lady Inglefield and Brigadier-General E.C.W.D. Walthall, the president and chairman of the infirmary's board of management.

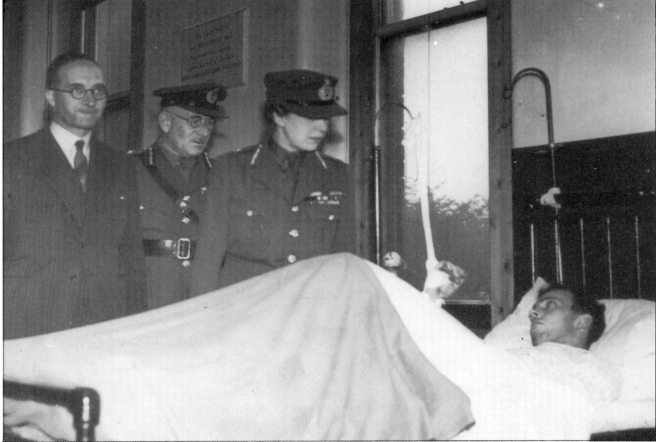

A regular royal visitor to Derby over the years was Princess Mary, the Princess Royal, sister of George VI. She is seen in ATS uniform on a visit to Derbyshire Royal Infirmary in 1944 to talk to wounded soldiers.

In May 1955, the Duchess is received by the Marquess of Lothian at Melbourne Hall.

In November 1951, the Princess Royal is met at
Derby Midland Station by Sir Ian Walker-
Okeover, the Lord Lieutenant of Derbyshire. She
was here as president of the YMCA Women's
Auxiliary for a ceremony at the King's Hall,
receiving purses of money raised for the YMCA.
Her visit in April 1963 was for a similar occasion
at Derby Playhouse, the money going towards
the building of Derby's new YMCA centre. With
her is Mayor Stuart Harper.

The Duke of Kent, youngest brother of George VI, made a wide-ranging tour of Derby on 5 March 1941. He is seen here with workers at International Combustion and then chatting with war-worker Molly Chambers at Bliss and Co.

The Duke of Kent talked to the Chief Constable, Captain (later Colonel) Rawlings and Chief Air Raid Warden Mr T. Walton before inspecting Civil Defence personnel, uniformed and (opposite, top) not quite uniformed.

King George and Queen Elizabeth made a surprise visit to Derby on 8 August 1940 — it was a secret until shortly before their arrival by train. No crowds were out to see them until the news had spread and the royal visitors were returning to the station. This picture of the King at Rolls-Royce seeing work on a Merlin engine was approved by the Ministry of Information and passed by two censors before it could be published with a caption reduced to: 'The King inspecting an engine when he visited a Derby factory today.'

When Princess Elizabeth married Philip Mountbatten in November 1947 there was no television in the homes of Derby. Film of the wedding was eagerly awaited and people flocked to the town's cinemas to watch it.

The flags were out on Monday 27 June 1949 when Princess Elizabeth, the future Queen, and the Duke of Edinburgh came to town, principally to open the new Derby Council House but also to carry out several other engagements. This was St Peter's Street in festive mood.

The Princess at Royal Crown Derby watches plate decorators at work and at Rolls-Royce offices in Nightingale Road she turns to comment to the Duke after studying the Battle of Britain memorial window.

"Whereas it hath pleased Almighty God to call to . . ." The proclamation of the death of George VI and accession of Elizabeth II is read by the High Sheriff of Derbyshire, Mr G.C.M.Jackson from the steps of the Shire Hall in St Mary's Gate on 9 February 1952.

Perhaps the queues were not so long as in 1935 on the death of George V but the feeling was as sincere as Derby people went to the Council House to view the town's wreath for the funeral of George VI.

Police sergeants W.Pickering (Derby Borough) and R.Metcalf (Derbyshire) went to Windsor as local police representatives at the funeral of the King.

To coincide with the funeral of King George VI at St George's, Windsor, a civic service was conducted at Derby Cathedral. Crowds lined the streets for the procession in which the Mayor, Councillor Zachariah Grayson, was preceded by the sword and maces.

Derby Market Place, 28 March 1957 and Elizabeth II, on her first visit to Derby as Queen, inspects the guard of honour as the civic dignitaries await her.

A wave from the balcony of the Council House, the building she had opened on her visit eight years earlier.

A massed reception by schoolgirls for the royal car at the Leylands Cottage Homes complex off Broadway.

"Who's that walking past my door?" A resident of the Leylands comes out to see.

Reminiscences about the Coronation service? The Queen went on from Derby to Repton where she met Lord Fisher, former Headmaster of Repton School and former Archbishop of Canterbury, the man who had crowned her four years before.

Signing in at the Council House, watched by the Mayor, Councillor William Bonell, is Princess Margaret. She was in St John Ambulance uniform for this visit in July 1965 because she was here as Commander-in-Chief of the St John Ambulance and Nursing Cadets and was presenting awards to cadets from all over the country at a parade at Bemrose School. It rained and the outdoor ceremony, with 7,000 people attending, was switched to inside the school.

An interlude of fine weather and the Princess walks through the lines of cadets. With her is Captain P.J.B.Drury-Lowe, the St John Ambulance Brigade County Commissioner.

# Civic Pride

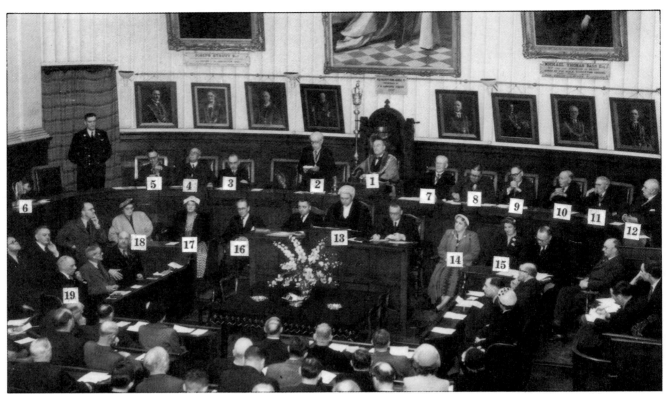

In 1953, Derby Town Council was still meeting in the old chamber in the Guildhall. This was the scene at the Mayor-making ceremony held there on 27 May 1953 with the father of the council, Alderman William Raynes, standing to propose the election of Councillor Henry Russell as Mayor. Others identified on the picture are: (1) the retiring Mayor, Councillor Thomas Dennis; (3) Alderman Arthur Sturgess; (4) Alderman David Butler; (5) Alderman Ernest Armstrong; (6) Alderman Thomas Johnson; (7) Alderman John Clark; (8) Alderman Herbert Hind; (9) Alderman Charles Bowmer; (10) Alderman A.R.Flint; (11) Alderman William Phillips; (12) Alderman George Warburton; (13) Mr E.H.Nichols, the Town Clerk; (14) Mrs Dennis, the retiring Mayoress; (15) Mrs Russell, the new Mayoress; (16) Mr Philip Noel-Baker, Derby South MP; (17) Mrs Noel Baker; (18) Mrs Wilcock, wife of Group Captain C.A.B.Wilcock, Derby North MP; and (19) the incoming Mayor.

Out of the old, into the new. It is 21 October 1954 and the first meeting of the Town Council in the new debating chamber. Although the Council House had been officially opened by Princess Elizabeth in June 1949, work on building the council chamber in the centre of the complex did not begin until several years later. Presiding is the Mayor, Councillor Alec Ling, with the bewigged Town Clerk, Mr G.H.Emlyn Jones, next to him. Standing to declare the official opening of the chamber is father of the council Alderman William Raynes — the man after whom the Raynesway section of Derby ring-road was named.

The new municipal offices complex, the Council House as it was to be named, was 16 years in the building. This was the scene in August 1938, a month after the start of work on laying the foundations. In the background is the newly-completed police station and courts building.

It is March 1939 and the steel framework of the municipal building is well advanced. In this view from the top of the Cathedral tower, the new open market and the bus station can be seen in the background with the cattle market beyond to the left.

Well and truly laid. The Mayor, Alderman David Butler, lays the foundation stone of the new municipal offices in June 1939. Work was halted when World War Two began three months later.

Building work on the offices continued in March 1940 and the date 1941, in Roman numerals MCMXLI, appears on this classical columned pediment of the main entrance, seen as that part neared completion in June 1941. By August 1942 the building was sufficiently advanced for it to be requisitioned as offices for the RAF, continuing as such until April 1946. The post-war shortage of building materials meant further delays in completing the construction.

The family silver on display. The completion of the Council House came very opportunely on the 800th anniversary of Derby being granted its first charter by King John. It meant that the Corporation had true cause to receive gifts to furnish its new home and set up displays of civic treasures. So 1954 was declared Octocentenary Year — even though, to within a year or so, the date of the charter was unknown. The Corporation was showered with very acceptable gifts, mainly crested silverware, from commerce, industry and organisations in the town. Here the gifts are set out in the reception room where they are still displayed in glass cases.

In close-up, the silver tea and coffee set that was the gift of British Celanese.

Corporation charters have a lot to do with holding markets, so on the Octocentenary, the Mayor, Councillor Alec Ling, thought he ought to go on an inspection tour of the town's markets. He did so by stage coach, here seen setting out from the Council House.

Thousands lined the streets of Derby on Saturday, 2 October 1954, for what was described as a giant cavalcade, the highlight of the charter celebrations. The Mayor swapped his stage coach for an open 1907, made-in-Derby, Rolls-Royce Silver Ghost to ride in the procession to Markeaton Park. Note that in each case, the Mayor's Officer sits next to the driver, in uniform and bearing the mace on his shoulder.

The charter celebrations cavalcade moves along Albert Street with floats representing Derby industries and with men of the Derby Borough Fire Brigade riding on an ancient horse-drawn fire engine. Crowds on the pavements are six or seven deep for an occasion that brought some colour to a still rather drab post-war era of austerity.

They roasted a sheep in Markeaton Park and the Mayoress, Mrs Ling, receives her portion in a bread roll from the end of a sword. This was only three months after the official end of all food rationing.

Another civic practice which has fallen into disuse — unaccountably — since the 1960s is the bestowing of the honorary freedom of the ancient borough on people who have done long and outstanding service for Derby or the country. Here in March 1968 are the last three people honoured, long-serving Aldermen Matthew Lowe, Charles Bowmer and Alec Ling, pictured with Mayor Robert Stott and Town Clerk Norman Fisher (the last to hold that office, abolished in 1974). Since the 1830s there had been 31 honorary freemen, among them Lord Curzon of Kedleston (Viceroy of India), Field-Marshal Douglas Haig, Mrs Adeline Rivers (mother of Derby VC Private Jake Rivers) and, during World War Two, the then Prime Ministers of Canada (MacKenzie King), New Zealand (Peter Frazer), and South Africa (Jan Smuts) and the Chinese Ambassador. Others honoured included MPs and a dozen aldermen over the years.

From 1380 when Richard II accepted the Derby burgesses' plea to move the seat of Assizes from Sawley — midway between Derby and Nottingham — to Derby itself, the Assize judges sat in Derby three times a year for the 'general gaol delivery' of Derbyshire. The whole system of English courts changed when Crown Courts were set up in the early 1970s. The opening of Derby Assizes was always attended with ceremonial, including the judges processing for a service at Derby Cathedral from where in this 1963 picture, Mr Justice Finnemore emerges, pausing for a word with Provost Ronald Beddows. In the background is Dr W.R.C.Chapman, Cathedral warden and long-time headmaster of Bemrose School.

# Along the Riverbank

The building of the Council House was the last project in the 1930s civic redevelopment scheme along the west bank of the Derwent. The first was the building of Exeter Bridge, seen here under a rather bizarre test during its construction in 1931. Would it take the weight of the traffic? This procession of traction engines, steam rollers and heavy lorries rumbled on to the half finished bridge to prove that it would. The bridge was officially opened by the then Minister of Transport, Herbert Morrison.

The approach to the new bridge is seen on the right in this picture which seems to have been taken from the top of another Derby's famed features, the Shot Tower, then nearing the end of its existence. Here we look down on the jumble of buildings soon to be cleared for the building of the Police Station and Courts complex and, in the foreground, those on the future Council House site.

Wide open spaces and room to walk with cyclists the only traffic in sight. It is January 1937 and the new Police Building looks pretty much as it will still look more than half a century hence in the 1990s.

An earlier source of civic pride along the river was the Derby Electric Power Station — even though it hid the historic Silk Mill and its chimneys vied with the ancient tower of the Cathedral. It was built in 1921 and here a party of official visitors are being shown around its wonders of power generation.

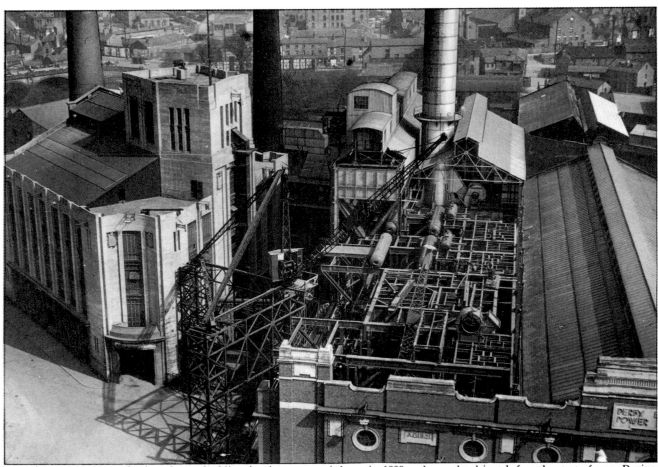

Extensions to the Power Station almost doubling its size were carried out in 1939 and completed just before the start of war. During the war the name Derby was covered over (see below) as were many names and direction signs, reportedly to confuse spies and escaped prisoners-of-war.

End of the era. The Power Station was demolished in 1971. Here crashing down is one of the 125ft chimneys — with the Silk Mill, later to house the Industrial Museum, once more emerging into view.

At the other end of the riverside development was another remarkable and long-standing feature of the Derby scene — the Long Bridge. In this scene from the 1930s, the wooden bridge is being used as a jumping-off point for young bathers in the Derwent. The unusual bridge was built as tow-path for horses drawing barges along Derby Canal, one arm of which crossed the river at that point on its way to Shelton Lock and beyond. Parts of the canal had already fallen into disuse but the bridge long continued as a convenient footpath for people crossing the river.

Derby Canal remained in private ownership, and in disuse, when canals were nationalised with the railways in 1947. The Long Bridge became in a dangerous state. This Closed notice went up in 1950.

By the end of 1959, this was all that remained of the Long Bridge. Now the weir, which ensured deeper water for the canal to cross the river, is the only reminder of that canal and its tow-path bridge.

Barges lie abandoned in the arm of the canal along by Stores Road. "It is nearly four years since there was any traffic on this part of the canal," records a note attached to this 1930 picture.

How much the canal was in use at the start of World War Two it is difficult to know, but here in September 1939 a barge returns with sand dredged from the river along the Long Bridge.

*Left and opposite page:* For more than a century the Shot Tower was a feature of the Derby skyline. It was built for bullets — or more precisely for lead shot for guns. The firm of Cox Brothers which made lead sheeting and pipes, from lead mined in Derbyshire, set up the tower at their works at the end of The Morledge. When it was built is not recorded, but it was certainly there in 1824. Molten lead poured through sieves at the top fell as drops inside the tower, becoming round and solidifying before they hit the reservoir of water at the bottom. It is not known when the tower was last in use, but it remained a landmark until the end of 1931. Here it is seen just before the start of demolition, then when part way down and finally almost gone. The name shot Tower Corner survived for another half-century until further demolitions at the corner of Albert Street and Tenant Street came with the refurbishing of the Market Hall. The actual site of the tower was somewhere between the present traffic island and the Council House car park.

A busy market scene at the Shot Tower end of The Morledge about the time of World War One.

Further back for the long view of The Morledge towards the end of the 1920s. Soon all the area to the right was to be cleared for the start of the Bus Station scheme and the making of the River Gardens and the open market that would replace those stalls stretching along the thoroughfare.

Down at ground level and just a few years later. Clearance has not yet started. The first thing to go will be that famous Shot Tower in the centre of the picture.

The Co-op Cow — another long-time and still surviving Derby landmark. It is not so well seen today as in this 1960 view when the long-empty corner site had still not been developed.

The Morledge Market moved but some street stalls remained on Cockpit Hill, across the road from the Bus Station, until cleared for the building of the Eagle Centre at the start of the 1970s. This is a scene from its final days.

The large building in the background of this picture of the Morledge Market (after demolition had started) is the Ice Factory, standing on what was to become Cock Pitt (*sic*) Island of the Inner Ring Road.

One of the most ancient buildings of Derby could well have been lost in the 1930s. St Mary's Chapel, the chapel-on-the-bridge, dates from the 14th century when the original wooden St Mary's Bridge was replaced by one of stone. The building was in a perilous state when this picture was taken in the 1920s. The last surviving pier of the medieval bridge can be seen under the chapel, just to the left of the balustrade of the 18th-century bridge which replaced it.

This was the inside of the chapel when restoration work began in 1930. In the middle of the 19th century the building had become a workshop and a house had been built on to it. The derelict property was acquired in 1928 by Derbyshire Archaeological Society and the restoration was funded by Mr Eric Haslam and his sisters as a memorial to their father, Sir Alfred Haslam.

The mason working on stones for the chapel restoration is identified as Mr John Cockayne, described as a member of the congregation 40 years before — suggesting that in the late 19th century the building had again seen use as a chapel. The stone he is using has come a short way from the Derwent Bridge that was then being demolished and replaced by the new Exeter Bridge.

St Mary's Bridge, Chapel and House as seen in 1941.

The bridge led into Bridge Gate, seen here in 1925, flanked by its two churches, St Mary's Catholic Church and the 19th-century St Alkmund's Church, last of several so dedicated to stand on that site. After Chesterfield's twisted version, this was the highest spire in Derbyshire. One story has it that the spire was built so high spitefully to mask St Mary's.

Because of danger of collapse and cost of repair, the top of the spire was removed in the 1960s, leaving St Alkmund's with a flat top and below the 200ft mark. The church was later demolished to make way for the inner-ring road which also sandwiched Bridge Chapel between St Mary's Bridge and a new bridge over the river.

# Through The Town, Down The Years

The Police Station, the offices of *Derbyshire Advertiser* and between them the Guildhall, looking from this view pretty much the same as it does today. With an open-top tram, a single-decker bus, landaus, bicycles, market stalls, the Bass statue . . .and people with time to stand and stare, this was Derby Market Place some time during the second decade of the century.

Move on a few years and the Market Place seems a place of more clutter. It is 1925 and the year after the unveiling of the War Memorial, which now stands surrounded by wreaths of poppies, but also by the market stalls with their boxes, barrels, bags of coal and carts. The near-derelict property in the background, on the corner of Irongate, will soon be cleared for the building of the Barlow Taylor department store, now Derbyshire Building Society's city offices.

At the other end of the Market Place, a policeman stands on a box to control traffic at the corner of Derwent Street. This is 1928 and all the propety on that side of Derwent Street will go for road widening. Departmental offices of the council are on the opposite side.

From about the same spot, but some years earlier, this was the view along Derwent Street, with a glimpse of the old Derwent Bridge in the distance.

The road-widening has taken place in this 1931 view. Only half of the building that stood on the corner now remains as Ramsden's Restaurant, next to the 18th-century Assembly Rooms. Also to be seen is the Boy and Goose statue, later moved to the River Gardens and now back not far from that original spot. It is inside the new Assembly Rooms complex, built in the 1970s after fire destroyed the old building in 1963.

The buntings are out in the Market Place for the celebration of the Silver Jubilee of George V in 1935. That end of the Market Place is now, the notice announces, a Motor Park with charges of 'cars 6d, charas 1/- for two hours' — which works out at about £1.25 and £2.50 at today's prices.

The Market Place at night in 1938 — a year to go before those lights would all be extinguished for the blackout in World War Two.

Also at the end of the 1930s, the Derby Corporation Public Health offices on the corner of Derwent Street and Tenant Street. Later the building was to become offices of Shardlow Rural District Council, forerunner of South East Derbyshire Rural Council.

The shops down the other side of Tenant Street survived into the 1970s when work also began, in the background, on building the new Assembly Rooms.

Before the infamous hole appeared — the site of aborted plans for an hotel — the old council offices still stood as shops and there was a pedestrian subway under Corporation Street. This was talked of as the site for a new library.

One of the oldest and most important thoroughfares of Derby — Irongate between the Market Place and All Saints' Church which in 1927 became Derby Cathedral. Today, with its commemorative obelisk at the site of the birthplace of artist Joseph Wright of Derby, it is a pedestrian zone. In this 1960 picture from the top of the Cathedral tower, it was still the A6, the London to Carlisle road, through the centre of town.

Not a lot has changed about Irongate in more than half a century. This was the view of it from outside the West door of the Cathedral in 1938. Most of it is entirely recognisable from the same spot today.

Looking in the opposite direction in 1959, only the traffic seems to have changed. In the background, beyond the Cathedral, the spire of St Alkmund's looms through the haze.

The continuation of Irongate to the south of the Market Place is Cornmarket. Here again we are in about the second decade of the century with cabs on rank, a tram passing and Boy Scouts apparently collecting for the lifeboat charity. Note the clock, the long-surviving feature of Cornmarket.

Again the challenge is to spot how Irongate changed between this view in 1934 and the one in 1948 when a horse-drawn cart could still make the leisurely turn into St James's Street.

We are into the 1950s and looking the opposite way down Cornmarket, towards Victoria Street and the St Peter's Street junction. Look closely to see the policeman on point duty opposite the end of St James's Street. Another policeman, on the pavement, seems about to take over the arm-waving from him. At most times there was a policeman directing traffic at this busy corner.

It is 1960. The policeman has gone — because it is Sunday — but the clock over the jewellers is still there. It will remain until 1968 when all those shops go to make room for the building of Littlewoods.

'The magnet that draws the people' and on the ends of the magnet, 'Quality and Cheapness'. That was the sign on the Midland Drapery, Derby's first and largest department store, on the corner of St Peter's Street and East Street and stretching quite a distance along each street. This picture is from about the 1920s looking down St Peter's Street from by the church, with Boots Cash Chemists on the opposite corner of East Street. Midland Drapery went in 1970; from first-floor level up, the Boots building with its statues in alcoves remains almost unchanged.

The view along St Peter's Street in the mid-1930s. Up on the right is Thurman and Malin's, a rival of Midland Drapery just across the road. But already appearing on the scene are the chain stores, Marks and Spencer's in their big new premises on the left (still much the same in the 1990s) and the Fifty Shilling Tailors with Freeman, Hardy and Willis's shoe shop on the right.

A busy shopping day in St Peter's Street in the spring of 1939 and then the street almost deserted on Easter Monday in 1960.

Looking down East Street from St Peter's Churchyard in the 1930s.

The Spot in 1939, with the traffic almost in procession. This was a favourite place for boards advertising entertainments and other events.

If Midland Drapery was St Peter's Street, Ranby's was definitely dominant in Victoria Street. The shop, with its roof-level boards reminiscent of a town in the Wild West, is seen behind the bus shelter in this 1930s picture.

Determindly tucked into the Ranby's complex at the corner of Victoria Street and Green Lane is the Queen's Head pub, seen here at the end of the 1950s, shortly before it was demolished for the full-scale rebuilding of Ranby's and its metamorphosis into Debenhams.

Looking like another intruder into the long line of Ranby's along Victoria Street was the Congregational Church, seen here shortly before World War Two. It was the third church on the site and it was demolished in 1961 as part of the Ranby's development, being replaced by a new church within the redevelopment.

One of Derby's key junctions — outside the Post Office where the Wardwick, the Strand, St James's Street and Victoria Street meet. The outline of the buildings stays the same over the years; the road layout goes through constant change. In this scene from the 1920s, tram, trolley bus and bicycles seem to have right of way.

At least three prams are to be seen as pedestrians stroll across the junction unhindered by traffic. The policeman on his stand surveys the 1920s scene.

The cobbles have gone, the first traffic island appears at the junction and the Wardwick is busy with buses. This is 1936.

Into the 1940s. More street 'furniture' but traffic lights have yet to come here. Derby's first traffic lights, robots as they were then called, were set up in St Peter's Street in 1929.

Sadler Gate Bridge at the end of the 1920s when Cheapside was a bus terminus and the buses used this space to make U-turns. To get your bearings, look at the building beyond that with the large sign T.P.Townsend. This is now the end building of Sadler Gate and it still bears the nameplate Sadler Gate Bridge, seen in the picture between the left-hand pair of first-floor windows. The car on the left is a chain-driven Trojan, a model that was praised for its reliability if not its appearance.

Move up into Sadler Gate, a picture taken at around the same date.

Move further up and go
on a few years. This was
the scene in the 1930s.

By the 1950s traffic was becoming a problem in narrow Sadler Gate but the shopkeepers could make light of it, acquiring a great reputation for their Christmas lights, seen here in 1968.

# Here and There About Town

Derby's first theatre, in Bold Lane, has gone through many owners and many uses in its 220 years. It was built as a theatre in the 1770s. In this 1934 picture it was probably still in use to some extent as the Gospel Hall which the façade inscription (soon after removed) records it became in 1865. Later it was acquired by the County Council, used as a library and then as a magistrates' court.

A dog can bask in the sunshine of the almost traffic-free Curzon Street in this view from the 1930s. The Temperance Hall, built in the 1850s, was then still used as such. Later it was to become the Churchill Hall, headquarters of Derby Conservative Association, and it is now the Elim Pentecostal Church.

In Friar Gate in 1936 the 18th-century Unitarian Chapel (earlier Presbyterian) stands next to the Friary Hotel. The Friary was the home of the Boden family until it became an hotel about 15 years before this picture was taken. Although twice extended since, it still appears much the same from this angle — less the iron railings which, with those of the chapel, went in the World War Two salvage drive. The chapel was demolished for the building of the Heritage Gate offices complex in the 1970s with a replacement chapel set amidst the offices.

Across the road the flags are out for the Coronation in 1953. The shops at ground level change; above not much is different.

The clock provides the clue to where this is. The clock, itself renovated in recent years, is still on that end wall on the corner of Ford Street and Friar Gate. Gone is the Queen Anne house standing derelict in this 1938 picture. The widened Ford Street and a car park now fill the space.

Not a lot of change now from this 1960 view of the Georgian properties along Friar Gate. It seems that just the creeper has crept away.

Into the by-ways and this is one with a remembered name. It is Becket Well Lane, swept away with the ancient well itself when the Duckworth Square shopping precinct was built, off Victoria Street, in 1963.

Becket Well, seen here in 1959, was a survivor of the medieval wells of Derby; another was St Alkmund's Well. This stone capping was put on Becket Well in the 17th century when it became part of George Sorocold's pioneering piped water system for the town. It was in use until the mid-19th century. The capping is said to survive in a garden somewhere in the Derby area.

Albert Street, probably in the 1920s. Certainly before September 1929 when the green domed Palace Theatre became the offices and printing house of the *Derby Evening Telegraph*. It was built as the Corn Exchange in 1861 and that was the name it reverted to when the *Telegraph* moved out and the building became shops and a snooker hall in the early 1980s.

Babington Lane in the May sunshine of 1930 with the sunblinds out to protect the displays in the windows of Brindleys, drapers and hosiers. Further up the street is the Grand Theatre with its twice-nightly presentation of the top touring stage shows.

East Street in December 1963, busy with Christmas shoppers and with traffic before the coming of pedestrianisation and the demolition down the right-hand side for the building of the Eagle Centre Market.

Becket Street Drill Hall, so-called even though its main entrance was in Newland Street. It was built for the Volunteers in the 1860s and at the time of this 1939 picture it was still very much in use by the Sherwood Foresters of the Territorial Army, despite the fact that it appeared to be boarded up — the war had started and this was the first tentative efforts to protect it from enemy action. The hall was also much used for non-military purposes. The reception to celebrate Derbyshire winning the County Cricket Championship was held there in 1936 and through into the 1960s it was used for social occasions, exhibitions and various other events. It was beaten by the enemy within — demolished to make way for new Department of Health and Social Security offices, Forester House.

St Andrew's, the railwaymen's church in London Road, was built in 1867 to the designs of Sir Gilbert Scott who was also working on a project at the other end of the Midland Railway line, designing St Pancras Station in London. The church was actually in Litchurch, a town in its own right until absorbed into Derby in 1878. It is seen here in the 1930s. In the 1960s it was declared redundant and was demolished in 1970, but its name lives on in St Andrew's House, another office of the Department of Social Security. It is an odd fact that three Derby churches demolished about that time — St Alkmund's, St Andrew's and Victoria Street Congregational — all had spires; now there is not one tall spire left in Derby; about the tallest is that of the former Christ Church, Normanton Road, now the Serbian Orthodox Church of the Holy Apostles Peter and Paul.

Tallest tower? No doubts about that. The Perpendicular tower of All Saints' Church, now Derby Cathedral, was built in the early 16th century. It is 212ft high and was claimed to be the second highest church tower in the country, after Boston Stump. This 1930s picture shows the East end of the building designed by James Gibbs and built on to the tower in 1725 after the rest of the medieval church was demolished.

The 1968 extension to the Cathedral nearing completion. An extension was first planned when the church became the Cathedral in 1927 but it was not until the arrival of Provost Ronald Beddows in 1952 that plans began to move towards reality.

St Werburgh's Church in the 1930s. The AA finger-post shows the way to London and the South and to Ashbourne and Manchester but the traffic lights, possibly newly installed, do not seem to be working.

A tram comes down the hill from Nottingham Road Cemetery. The date is before 1923 because the tram is on a single track. It was after the high ground on the edge of the cemetery collapsed early in 1923 that the road was widened and a double track was laid down.

Another tram rounds the corner out of Kedleston Road at the Five Lamps junction. Just behind the front of the tram can be made out the ornate standard bearing five lamps. Whether this was the original which gave the junction its name and how long it remained is not clear.

A famous junction on the other side of town — the Cavendish. It is here seen, under a maze of trolley wires, in 1954.

Kingsway Drill Hall under construction during the summer of 1939. War was only a few months away. The building was to be the headquarters of the 68th Anti-Aircraft Brigade of the Territorial Army.

Midland Road Post Office, on the corner of Carrington Street, in 1939. Extensions to the building had been going on for 40 years. Further plans were halted by the war but the Post Office complex expanded along Midland Road after the war.

A Derby landmark rising. The 120ft water tower off Radbourne Lane was being built in 1947 to supply the vast Mackworth Estate development, one of the first and largest of Derby's post-war housing schemes.

Find your way round the centre of Derby in the 1920s. In this early aerial picture, the junction of Cornmarket, Victoria Street, St Peter's Street and Albert Street is in the centre at the bottom. The Derwent flows across the top of the picture.

They called it the new arterial road. It was the grand scheme for through traffic to bypass Derby. It was part of Derby's great development scheme of the 1930s and although the complete circle around Derby was never completed — again the war was to blame — the idea was well ahead of its time. Here in September 1938, Mayor Edward Paulson is declaring open the dual-carriageway section between Chaddesden and Alvaston which was to be known as Raynesway. The opening, using gold scissors, should have been performed by the Minister of Transport, Leslie Burgin, but he could not get away from London. The opening coincided with the Munich crisis.

Two sections of the ring-road, Broadway and part of Kingsway, completed and ready for opening. Although only single carriageway, allowance had been made for expansion into dual carriageway.

A motor-cycling family, with side-car, experience the traffic-free
pleasures of the newly opened Kingsway section of ring-road.

From the top of the Cathedral tower in the summer of 1939. Victoria Street Congrational Church is in the middle distance on the
left, the tower of Derby Library, Museum and Art Gallery in the centre and the tower of St Luke's Church, Stockbrook Street, is in
the distance on the right.

A 1960s view from over Bridge Gate, with St Alkmund's spire in its foreshortened state. The old Great Northern railway line runs down the right-hand side from Friar Gate at the top. The programme of clearance has begun in Queen Street and King Street.

Main Centre, the first of the central shopping developments is in the centre of this 1964 view, with Traffic Street, first section of the inner ring-road leading to the newly completed Bradshaw Way section on the left.

We are over Little City with Babington Lane and Green Lane leading up from the bottom edge. It is 1966 and across St Peter's Street some clearance for building Eagle Centre has begun with the open space turned into car parks.

# *Learning and Leisure*

St Peter's Parochial Hall, pictured here in its 1940s state, was an original building of Derby Free Grammar School — Derby School — set up by Queen Mary I in 1554 and believed to be one of the first endowed schools in the country.

It was in the 1860s that Derby School moved from St Peter's Churchyard to St Helen's House, King Street, which had been the home of William Strutt. This 1930s picture shows the original block with the Old Derbeians' War Memorial outside the main door.

91

The school took a stern pride in military tradition, exemplified in its Combined Cadet Force, seen here on parade in 1954, being inspected by Lord Alexander of Tunis.

After just over a century at St Helen's House, the school moved to new premises at Moor Lane, Littleover — and they took with them their War Memorial, seen being dismantled in March 1966. Now it is back in its original place; Derby School ceased to be in 1989, the end of 430 years' history. The memorial was returned to St Helen's House which had by then become an adult education centre.

After Derby School (nearly 300 years after), the National School had claim to be the oldest in Derby. It was established in 1812 in Bridge Street, moved to Bold Lane after a fire in 1817 and finally to here in Curzon Street in 1842. This was the building in 1951, not long before its demolition.

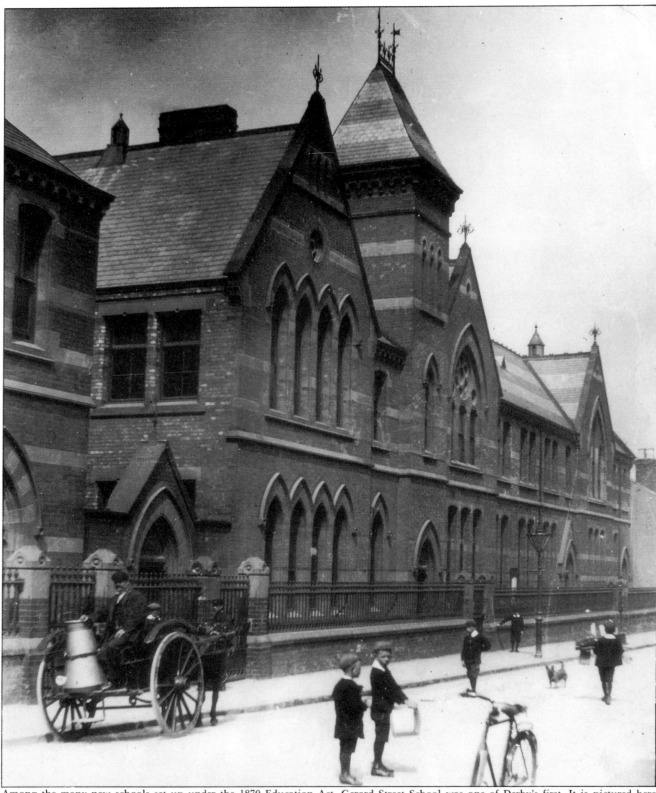

Among the many new schools set up under the 1870 Education Act, Gerard Street School was one of Derby's first. It is pictured here during the early part of the century. It changed its name to Becket School after World War Two and was demolished in 1974, just about on its centenary.

Being demolished in 1968 is King's Mead School, another of the 1870 Act's Board Schools as they were known, having first been administered directly by boards set up for that purpose, rather than by the Borough Council, which took over control of them in 1906.

Another built in 1842 was the Diocesan School at the corner of Friar Gate and Vernon Street, pictured here in 1939. The building later became part of the private Vernon High School and then was converted into a social club.

More schools meant a need for more teachers. Before the 1870 Act most of the schools were set up by churches, some of them just Sunday schools. So it was Lichfield Diocese (of which Derby was then part) that opened the Uttoxeter New Road college 'For the Training of School Mistresses' in the 1850s. The building, seen here in 1960, continued in use as ancillary college premises long after the building at Mickleover in the 1960s of Bishop Lonsdale Teacher Training College, named after the bishop who initiated plans for the original college. That still stands as a business centre.

Parkfields Cedars School in Kedleston Road was established as the Municipal Secondary School for Girls in 1917. It was centred on an early 19th-century house and was, indeed, flanked by cedar trees. This is a 1954 picture of the school, showing the original house and part of the extensions built on during the years.

The Uttoxeter New Road college was Derby's first establishment of higher education. Second, in 1878, was Derby School of Art in Green Lane, seen in this 1939 picture after several extensions to the original building. Later it was to be named after Derby's famed 18th-century artist, Joseph Wright. It is now part of Derby University and the buildings also house the Metro Cinema.

The impressive main staircase of Parkfields Cedars is seen before its total destruction by fire in February 1965.

Bemrose School in Uttoxeter Road was built in 1930 and named after Sir Henry Bemrose, whose home had been nearby. The school, seen with sandbagged windows in this wartime picture, developed from the Municipal Secondary School for Boys which Abbey Street School had become when the girls moved out to Parkfields Cedars.

Some of Derby's parks evolved from the grounds of the mansions on the edges of the town. Not so the Arboretum. This was created by the landscape gardener John Claudius Loudon. It was a gift to the town by Joseph Strutt, Derby's first Mayor after the Reform Act of 1835. It was the first public park in the country, opened with great ceremony in September 1840. This young visitor poses at one of the main intersection of paths on a summer's day during the second decade of this century when the fabulous park with its thousand trees was already 75 years old.

The same fountain at about the time that the Arboretum reached its centenary. The statue of Sir Henry Royce stands on its original site, unveiled in 1923, ten years before the death of the great car designing genius who always described himself simply as 'a mechanic'. The statue was moved to the Riverside Gardens in 1972 and is now outside the Derby headquarters of Rolls-Royce.

The Florentine Boar sculpture was a feature of the Arboretum from, probably, its opening until it disappeared during World War Two. This picture was taken in 1932. It was believed to be the work of William Coffee, who enjoyed the patronage of the Strutt family.

These guns, relics of previous wars, also went from the Arboretum during World War Two, possibly in the drive to turn any salvagable metal into guns, planes and tanks.

Young girls with prams, some containing dolls but most of them baby brothers or sisters. This is an early scene from Normanton Recreation Ground with its swings and, in the background, what appears to be an old tram to play in. A park-keeper, with stick, is to be seen in the centre.

Also at Normanton and about the same time. The ladies take a stroll in the sunshine. Father has been left to take care of the baby.

The decaying mansion of the Wilmot family, Osmaston Hall, is seen at the start of its demolition in September 1938. The whole estate was bought by the Midland Railway in 1888; they used part to build their carriage and wagon works and sidings and the hall itself was used for storage by the Midland's successors, the LMS. The parkland, on part of which five Royal Shows were held, the last in 1933, was variously used by Rolls-Royce, for housing, for golf and, more recently, for the development of Ascot Drive Industrial Estate. The only part to survive is the south-western corner that became the municipal Osmaston Park in 1922.

On the swings at Chester Green during the 1920s.

Daffodils at Darley Park. The hall, seen in the background of this 1941 picture, was the home of the Evans family until the end of the 1920s. It was used by Derby Central School until the late 1950s and was demolished in 1962.

Messing about on the river and playing cricket on Darley Fields. The scene in 1948.

Another park, another stately mansion — another demolition. This was Markeaton Hall, home of the Mundy family from 1775 until the last of the line, Emily Mundy, died in the 1920s. Even from the end of the 19th century, parts of the parkland had been made over for the public recreation. Now all of it was acquired by the borough and the lake was enlarged for boating. Military occupation during World War Two left scars on the park and on the hall which was eventually demolished in 1964, a few years after this picture was taken.

An oasis of peace in the town centre — this was St Peter's Churchyard in about the 1920s.

Fun in the streets. The Hospital Carnival, raising funds for hospitals was always a highly popular summer event between the wars. Here in the mid-1920s a Trent Motor Traction Co tableau moves through the crowds in the Market Place.

Boden's Pleasance was a small park in Bold Lane where the multi-storey car park now stands. The last reminder of it is this monument to Henry Boden which was part of its surround and still stands on the grass in front of the car park. In this 1950s picture some wartime construction survives behind it. Boden was a lace manufacturer and Derby temperance campaigner who lived at the Friary. When he died in 1908, his widow gave the 'pleasance' in his memory 'for the perpetual enjoyment of the citizens of the town,' as the plaque records. It became a children's recreation ground with swings in the 1920s and deteriorated into a badly neglected state long before it disappeared under the car park.

A spot that has improved with the years. This was the garden between the Library, Museum and Art Gallery and the backs of Cheapside in the 1920s. The museum extension of the 1960s came in the background to the right. The area, now known as Museum Square, has been re-landscaped several times over the years, the latest now in 1993.

From Congregational Church to Coliseum Cinema — and then to inner ring-road traffic island. This was the 1939 view of the cinema at the junction of London Road and Traffic Street where all changed in the 1960s.

Derby's first cinema opened in Babington Lane during the summer of 1910 and was still known by its long name of the Midland Electric Theatre when this picture was taken some years later.

Recognisably the same cinema but now called the Picture House with Mickey Rooney starring in 1939. After the war it became the Ritz, showing saucy 'Continental' films, and closed in the 1960s.

The Alexandra Cinema, or just the Alex, in Normanton Road was converted from a Victorian skating-rink and continued as a cinema until 1953 when for a short time it was a skating-rink again before becoming the Trocadero Ballroom. It was later a bingo hall and was destroyed by fire in 1982.

The Empire strikes back — or it did in the form of the Black Prince. Derby's second cinema to open, shortly after the Midland in 1910, was the Victoria Electric Theatre in Becket Well Lane. This picture was taken when it closed briefly at the outbreak of World War Two. After the war it was modernised and became the Black Prince, seen below in the 1950s after becoming Derby's first Cinemascope screen. It was demolished a few years later to make way for Duckworth Square shopping precinct and its replacement across the road, the Superama and then the Odeon Pennine, lasted only ten years.

In the big cinema-building boom of the 1930s, the Regal in East Street was the leader for the ABC group, pictured here in 1939 with a uniformed attendant outside ready for queue control — "Three seats in the one-and-threes" — when the cinema filled up later in the day.

The rival around the corner, in St Peter's Street, was the Odeon, another of the great picture palaces of the 1930s. This is a view from the 1950s. Ten years later it went in the start of the Eagle Centre development and the name Odeon was moved to what had been the Gaumont in London Road. In 1993 that is the only one of those great cinema buildings still standing — even though no longer a cinema.

Just how big those cinemas were can be gauged from this screen-eye-view of the auditorium of the Regal. This was reduced to smaller auditoria before it closed in 1984.

Built in 1928, and seen here in the 1940s, was the Popular in Mill Street. It closed in 1958 and a few years later began its chequered career as a theatre club, first highly successful under the name Talk of the Midlands and bringing star names of international show business to Derby.

The suburbs also had cinemas built on the grand style. Here was the Gloria in Nottingham Road, Chaddesden, shortly after it was built in 1938. It became the Essoldo 13 years later and from the mid-1970s it was variously a bingo hall and cinema.

The Hippodrome in Green Lane was never a direct rival to the Grand. It was of that lower order of theatre, a variety house, a music hall. It was opened in 1913 and this was how it appeared in 1937. It later became a cinema but returned to stage presentations in 1951 after the closure of the Grand by the company that now owned both. It became a bingo hall in the 1960s. The Hippodrome's claim to fame is that Flanagan and Allen wrote their song *Underneath the Arches* in a dressing-room there, a fact confirmed, shortly before his death, by Chesney Allen who, however, denied the rider to the story, that they were inspired to write the song by seeing the railway arches in Ford Street.

Bold Lane was Derby's first theatre but the Grand was quite rightly the grandest. It was conceived by impresario Andrew Melville, opened in March 1886 and was burned down, except for the front façade, six weeks later. It was re-built and re-opened in the November. This picture shows it not long before its closure in 1950. It remained empty for seven years, was converted into a dance hall by Mecca and has since undergone various conversions and name changes as a night-spot.

Inside the Grand, towering up from stalls to dress-circle, balcony and gallery. It did not change greatly over its 64 years as a theatre; this was 1936.

Derby Playhouse arose from a popular movement to set up a repertory theatre in the town. It began in 1948 as the Little Theatre in Becket Street and moved to this former Baptist Sunday School in Sacheverel Street in 1952. This was the theatre when ready for its opening production, J.B.Priestley's *When We Are Married*. It presented weekly rep, surviving a devastating fire that closed it for a year; it progressed to fortnightly, then three-weekly productions, closing in 1975 when the new Derby Playhouse was built in the Eagle Centre. The old building became an Asian cinema, the Ajanta, for two years, stood empty for longer and was finally demolished in 1989.

# The War Years

Before the lights went out for six years. The outbreak of war on 3 September 1939 meant total blackout of all lights in streets and from all buildings — as a protection from night-time air-raids. This was the scene over the Morledge and Derby Bus Station one night in July 1939 just before a test switch-off in preparations for the war that now seemed inevitable. A few minutes later not a light was to be seen.

Preparations for war had been going on for a long time — before and still after Chamberlain's return from Munich with the promise of 'peace for our time' in the autumn of 1938. This was six months after the Munich agreement — the National Service office in Derby Market Place in National Service Week during which the campaign was stepped up to draw in volunteers for full-time or part-time military service and also for ARP (Air Raid Precautions) work, forerunner of Civil Defence.

As the lights went out the sandbags went up. The sandbags were to protect buildings from the blast of bombs. These seem to be making sure that the Station Master at Derby LMS Station stays safe.

In London, sandbags protected the Prime Minister at 10 Downing Street. And they also protected 10 Downing Street, Derby, the actual address of an ARP wardens' post. Chamberlain was well known for his umbrella, so there was one of those here, too.

Run for the shelters. It is 1 September, Friday morning at Qualcast Ltd, Derby and in an air-raid evacuation practice they managed to clear the factory of its 800 employees in just three minutes.

Carrying your gas mask! Gas in air-raids was the great fear at the start of the war. The issue of gas masks began in 1938 before the Munich crisis. Here children of the Beaufort Street area are being fitted with gas masks at St Mark's Church Hall. When war began everybody had to carry their gas maks everywhere they went. The cardboard boxes in which they came did not last long and containers of many kinds were produced.

More blackout measures. In London Road, a Derby policeman in white, even to his helmet; a hood fixed over a Keep Left bollard so that its light can be seen only from directly in front (similar hoods went over car headlights); white bands painted round lamp standards to make them more visible in the dark; and a coating of paint over the windows of railway carriages.

The building of air-raid shelters, including household ones in the back garden, was another part of the preparation for war. In this March 1939 picture corrugated iron sections for shelters have arrived by rail at St Andrew's Wharf and are being loaded on to lorries for taking them to where they will be constructed.

Old wine vaults in Colyear Street are being converted into a public air-raid shelter that should accommodate several hundred people.

This is a shelter combined with an ARP wardens' post being built into an old cellar at the corner of Abbey Street and Monk Street — and drawing some interested spectators.

Petrol brand names immediately disappeared. It was all Pool Petrol and rationing began a fortnight after the start of the war. The price of 1s 6d a gallon was equivalent to today's 7p. Later, petrol for authorised commercial use was coloured red so that checks could be made on its illegal use.

Motorists queue at Derby Borough Motor Taxation Department to fill in the forms and collect their first petrol ration books.

War brought queues for many things. This one is for military service — no longer by volunteers. Compulsory military service began immediately with men being required to register, according to age, at their local Employment Exchanges, as these are doing in Normanton Road. This was soon followed by medical examination and then call-up to Army, Navy or Air Force.

A queue for the cinema. Immediately on the outbreak of war the Home Secretary ordered the closure of all places of entertainment. The ban did not last long. After only a week it was relaxed for cinemas outside big town centres. Here patrons queue at the Gloria, Chaddesden on its reopening. Note the gas masks in their original boxes.

Queuing for bread and cakes in East Street. This was 1941 and food shortages were now being felt severely. Rationing of basic foodstuffs had been in operation since January 1940. Strangely enough, bread itself was not rationed until after the war. Clothes rationing began in 1941.

One way to help out the meagre rations was to eat out — at a British Restaurant. The Ministry of Food, through local authorities, set up restaurants in town centres to cater for everybody but principally for those who could not get a midday meal at a works canteen or school. This one with its patient queue was in Tenant Street and was called the City Restaurant. (Even in wartime, it seems, Derby was continuing its aspirations to become a city, not achieved until 1977.)

Even a queue for water. This is January 1941, a picture taken by a *Derby Evening Telegraph* photographer in, probably, Rosehill Street, but the rubber stamp of the Press and Censorship Bureau on the back orders that it is "Not to be published." So we can only guess why water is being delivered by tanker. The broken windows in the houses behind suggest a bombing raid and perhaps the water main has been fractured. All wartime newspaper photographs and news stories had to be approved by the Government censor.

An emergency supply of water is available, in the summer of 1941, from this tank set up outside an ARP Wardens' Post somewhere in the streets of Derby, perhaps the West End. Other types of Emergency Water Supply tanks were set up for fighting fires.

Strict controls were placed on raising livestock and slaughtering animals for meat. This was the scene at Derby Cattle Market on 9 January 1940, at the last fatstock sale until after the end of the war.

Waste not, want not. Hundreds of bins for food scraps were spread through the streets of Derby and householders were asked to keep such scraps separate from their other household waste. The scraps went for feeding pigs and poultry.

Newspaper tycoon Lord Beaverbrook was
appointed Minister for Aircraft Production
by Prime Minister Winston Churchill and he
launched an appeal for salvage of every
description. Waste paper is here being
unloaded at the council's Stores Road Depot
in October 1941.

Like a butler with the family silver, a
workman at Ford Street Depot receives
household metal items for the salvage drive.

The iron railings had to go. Perhaps the most lasting effect of the wartime salvage drive was the removal of iron railings from outside homes, factories, public buildings, parks . . .everywhere that they could be found. The whole appearance of streets was changed in the space of a few weeks. Most were never replaced after the war. Here the railings are being dismantled outside Gerard Street School.

And the children had to go — evacuated. During the course of the war, Derby was both a place from which children were evacuated to escape expected bombing and a place to which they were evacuated for safety. First they went — some not very far, some a very long way. This group of youngsters, whose parents had the contacts or the money, are on their way to 'the Dominions,' as it was said. They are at Derby Midland Station, in mid-August 1939, about to board the train that will take them to an undisclosed 'port of embarkation,' some to South Africa, some perhaps to Canada.

Monday, the day after the war started, and this gathering of Derby pupils of all ages is outside St Andrew's Church in London Road, ready for the journey to safer parts of Derbyshire, perhaps as far as North Wingfield, possibly only to Duffield.

Putting on a brave smile. They have their spare clothes in bags and parcels, their gas masks, their arm bands and their labels. But they don't know where they are going. They are just part of that exodus from Derby during the first weekend of September 1939.

The boys of Derby Central School took their desks with them. They are moving to their wartime home in the hall at Darley Abbey Park where, unlike many evacuees who moved back after a not very long time, the school was to be based throughout the war and for many years afterwards.

Many Derby children were evacuated to Ripley. These are pictured in Crossley Park soon after their arrival there.

Not all Derby children were evacuated. These are in the air-raid shelter under Queen Street Baths after their swimming session was interrupted for an air-raid drill. Chin in first when putting on your gas mask.

Some people were made to go — into internment. In the wave of fear over 'spies,' many foreign nationals in Britain, some of whom had lived in the country for long years, were interned on the Isle of Man. Here, in rather undignified style, women aliens in Derby, including nuns, are escorted by police through the streets to the Midland Station in May 1940.

The flow of evacuees in reverse. With the dangers of invasion if the Battle of Britain were lost, children were moved from the South-east coastal towns. This is a boys' school arriving to go to their wartime premises, somewhere in Derbyshire.

In the last years of the war, more children from London and the South-east were evacuated to Derby to escape the Germans' last frantic bombardment with the V1 flying bombs and the V2 rockets. Buses line up along Station Approach in July 1944 to take evacuees from London to homes in the Shardlow area.

More than 500 London evacuees, many of them mothers with young children, arrived in Derby one day in July 1944. Some are here at one of the rest centres set up to accommodate them until proper billets could be found.

Dig for Victory. As food supplies became less in the second and third years of the war, everybody was urged to grow as many vegetables as possible. Schools took over spare land for crops. Here in March 1941 boys of St John's School are on their way to work their allotment at Markeaton.

It wasn't all bad being a warden in the ARP. Wardens' posts were in some odd places but they had a club with a licensed bar at the one in Stockbrook Street.

They first called them the LDV, the local Defence Volunteers; then they became the Home Guard. Dad's Army is the way they've been remembered. Here was the formation of the LDV in Derby as volunteers responded to the call to attend a meeting in the yard of the police headquarters on 24 May 1940, soon after Churchill had become Prime Minister and just before the evacuation from Dunkirk began.

Kitting out the LDV with uniforms and weapons took some time. Here NCOs are on a field tactics exercise at Sinfin. They have uniforms and cap badges but, for lack of other insignia, some still need LDV arm bands.

The Auxiliary Fire Service, the AFS, was another part of Civil Defence. Units were set up to augment the full-time firemen — and firewomen — of the National Fire Service, the NFS. The equipment was often makeshift, such as these 'fire engines' at one of the Derby AFS stations.

The AFS took to the water with this fire float on the Derwent.

Out on an AFS training exercise and demonstration on Exeter Bridge.

When the AFS had some new equipment they were proud to demonstrate it. Here, in 1941, members of the Borough Council's Watch Committee see the latest in foam extinguishers.

The National Fire Service set up a Derby training school in Radbourne Street where, in March 1943, firewomen are seen learning control-room practice.

Another branch of National Service was the Women's Land Army. Agriculture and food production was vital war work and the Land Army was formed to help farmers, many of whose workers were away fighting. Here a Land Army girl drives the tractor bringing in the hay at a Kirk Langley farm.

All hands to the harvest with a traction engine driving the threshing machine for the 1940 harvest at Mackworth.

Sheep safely graze . . .on the Municipal Sports Ground on a chill morning in 1940. Raising meat production as well as turning pastures to crops meant bringing into use any spare grazing ground.

Fears of invasion in the summer of 1940 led to guarding open spaces on which enemy planes might try to land. Old cars were spread about on Darley Fields.

War work for everybody. The girls here are making sand cores for vehicle castings at the iron foundry of Ley's Malleable Castings.

Instead of railway rolling stock, bodies for Lancaster bombers. This was a scene in the LMS workshops where aircraft, tanks and guns were produced as well the usual rail stock.

The British can keep smiling. This is a 1940 Christmas Eve concert in the air raid shelter of Abbey Street School.

The Russians came to see the war work. This sombre line-up is a delegation from the Soviet Union visiting Rolls-Royce and British Celanese in January 1942.

Derby went into the Army — and the Army came to Derby. This was the peacetime Army on parade at Normanton Barracks in the summer of 1938, knowing that it could not be long before war came.

They are joining the Army. Volunteers arriving through the gates of Normanton Barracks during the summer of 1939 and speedily collecting uniforms and kit from stores.

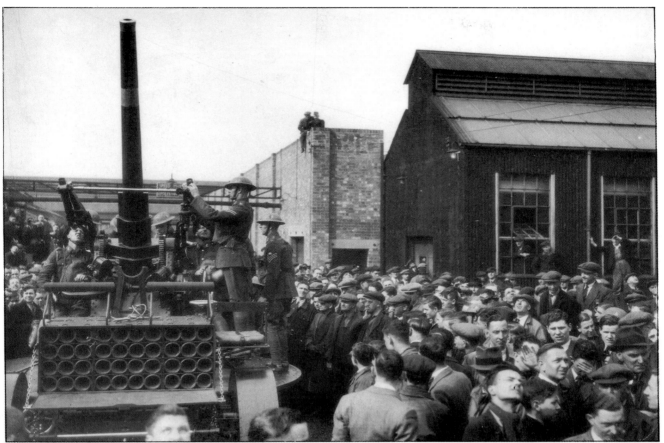

An anti-aircraft gun on display at Rolls-Royce works in 1938 for a demonstration of what could happen when war started and if the works were air attacked.

A sentry stands guard at the entrance to Markeaton Park. Behind are the roofs of the Royal Artillery Depot that had been established there. The date is December 1940.

Anti-aircraft gun batteries were set up at Derby Racecourse, concrete walls and sandbags round each emplacement, with camouflage nets for covering them. Note the barrage-balloon site in the background.

It was a fairway of the Markeaton Park pitch and putt course. Now it is a path lined with the depot's brick buildings and barrack blocks. They look as though they have come to stay. In fact, some of the buildings put up then were still there 50 years later with a car park on what had been the depot parade ground.

The cookhouse, with outdoor ovens, and Nissen huts at the Markeaton Park Depot.

Artillerymen under training at Markeaton Park loosening up in the depot gymnasium. Although these pictures were taken in 1940, they were subject to censorship and some were not published until 1945.

Soldiers everywhere you look . . .if you are allowed to look. This is dinner-time for men of the Royal Tank Corps at the Railway Orphanage, off Ashbourne Road.

Another takeover by the Army was at Alvaston. This is a view across the parade ground and sports field of the Royal Engineers' tented camp there in the summer of 1940.

At what was then known as the Railway College of the LMS at Alvaston — later the School of Transport — Royal Engineers get a practical lesson in running a railway, using the large model railway with complete signalling equipment which was still in use there for many years after the rail nationalisation.

Chapattis at Shirley. Indian troops came to the Derby area during the summer of 1940 and built their own camp, with their own catering, near Shirley and Osmaston.

Punjabi soldiers digging in at their Shirley camp, learning how to dig trenches for the kind of warfare there had been in World War One. King George VI went out to meet the Indians during his surprise visit to Derby in August 1940.

Save to win the war. People were constantly urged to put their money into National Savings to pay for the war effort. Special weeks were organised with towns setting targets for money raised for specific uses — Spitfire Week, Navy Week, Salute the Soldier Week or, in this case, War Weapons Week, in November 1940 with Sir Neville Henderson, Britain's former Ambassador in Berlin, launching it at a public meeting in Derby Market Place.

The feared full-scale blitz on Derby never came. The town suffered many minor bombing raids and was prepared for a big one. Here in January 1941, councillors are on an inspection tour of the emergency feeding and rest centres, this one in the Osmaston Park Road area. On the left is the Superintendent Relieving Officer, Mr T.Longdon.

Barrage balloons played a part in the defence of the town — the balloons and the cables trailing from them prevented low-level flying — but sometimes the balloons brought their own problems. In this October 1939 incident in Dean Street, a balloon that broke its mooring is recaptured and hauled down.

The first air-raid on Derby — damage done to houses in Jackson Avenue, Mickleover, by a small bomb that dropped in the back garden during the night of 24-25 June 1940. A woman living in the house on the right (a Mrs Henson, but the censor suppressed her name) was injured as she ran to the air-raid shelter; she later died.

Shoppers leave the air-raid shelters at the Municipal Buildings after a raid alert in August 1940. In all there were nearly 150 air-raid warnings in Derby during the six years of war, but few brought actual bombing of the town. Rolls-Royce, an obvious prime target, was bombed only once and that by a lone daylight raider in July 1942.

They came out unhurt. The censor was happy to let it be published that the occupants of this house, bombed in August 1940, escaped. But he would not allow it to be said the house was in Regent Street, Derby, merely in 'a Midlands town'.

Blast damage to a stand at the Baseball Ground in another August 1940 raid.

A boost to morale was provided by this shot-down enemy plane, put on display in Normanton Park in October 1940.

Derby's worst night of the war was 15-16 January 1941, as seen by the damage in these following pictures. Later figures estimated 20 people were killed and nearly 50 injured with damage to over 1,500 homes in a raid by, according to German records, 49 aircraft dropping 59 tonnes of high-explosive bombs and 1,500 incendiaries. At least one of those bombs landed on the LMS station. Troops are here seen searching the rubble at the station next day.

Bomb craters in the road and roofs blasted off the houses in Derby Lane, Normanton.

A direct hit on a house in Offerton Avenue.

Back-garden shelters blown up in Kenilworth Avenue.

Damage to houses somewhere in Alvaston.

All that was left of the bandstand in the Arboretum, scene of many memories of band concerts in summer sunshine for generations of Derby people. The censor approved this picture for publication without, of course, revealing where it was.

Bring out the flags. It's all over. The end of the war had been in sight for several days and at last, on 8 May 1945, it was official. This was VE-Day — Victory in Europe Day. And this was the scene in Norman Street, Derby, typical of streets throughout the town where the flags and bunting miraculously appeared from somewhere.

It poured with rain in the middle of the day but it only dampened the flags, not the spirits. People were still out waving.

Street parties were quickly organised. The tables are out and the children, many of them born in wartime, tuck into the goodies. These scenes are in Leonard Street and Liversage Street.

More street parties in Somerset Street and Belgrave Street, all over the next few days.

The spirit of celebration led to the revival of the old custom of well-dressing in Derby where, unlike in the villages, it had declined for years before the war. This dressing of St Alkmund's Well, at the corner of Bath Street and Well Street, in May 1945 was the first for 20 years.

The end of the war meant that the security over the German prisoners-of-war could be relaxed and that they could come out of the prison camps to do some work while awaiting their repatriation. Here some are busy tending crops in a field off Ford Lane, Allestree.

Italian prisoners-of-war had been able to have similar freedom for
some time, particularly following the surrender of Italy in 1943. This
Italian is helping with land reclamation work at Twyford.

Time for the evacuees to go home. The Mayor of Derby, Councillor William H.Phillips, is at Derby Midland Station in June to see
off some of the London evacuees who came to Derby a year before to escape the danger of the V2 rockets.

A smile and a wave from the departing evacuees as their train pulls out.

Dancing in the streets. They had the VE celebrations, but still there had been the continuing war in the Far East. That ended with the Japanese surrender after the dropping of the atom bombs on Hiroshima and Nagasaki. This was the scene in Derby Market Place on 15 August 1945, VJ-Day — Victory over Japan Day.

The tables were out again for street parties. This time some dads could be there, still in uniform but getting some leave as they awaited their demob.

The war might be over but there was still food shortages and austerity — which would get worse. There were still queues, this one, on VJ-Day, for bread at a baker's in Cornmarket.

Some delayed their celebrations to combine them with Christmas parties in the hope that food supplies might be better. Leacroft Road residents are here at their victory party at Dairyhouse Road Methodist Schoolrooms in January 1946.

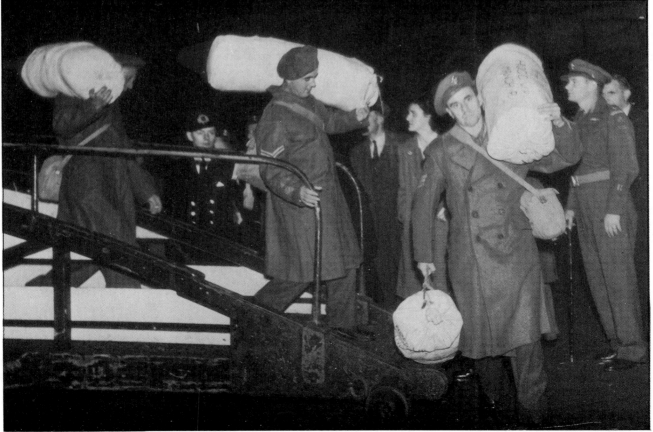

The soldiers are coming home. These Sherwood Foresters are setting foot in England again in October, on their way to Derby.

A lot has happened since they went away. Three Sherwood Foresters on their arrival at Derby Midland Station.

Just passing through. A train carrying former Far Eastern prisoners-of-war stops in Derby so that they can get out for some refreshments.

Demobbed soldiers would be looking for jobs. The LMS Loco Works in Derby would be wanting workers. A group of former prisoners-of-war from Germany are shown around by the works superintendent, Mr J.Rankin. They were the first of about 30 groups visiting the works during September 1945.

Derby marked the coming of peace with a Thanksgiving Week in October 1945. These ATS girls reach the saluting base on a march-past in the Market Place.

A guard of honour during Thanksgiving Week is inspected by Derby industrialist Sir J.Arthur Aiton, chairman of the organising body. In fact this was another of those National Savings Weeks such as there had been during the war. Derby's target of £1-m put into savings during the week was just surpassed.

"Now thank we all our God . . ." The Mayor, Councillor William H.Phillips, leads the town's thanksgiving at a VJ-Day service in Derby Cathedral. The sermon was delivered by the Bishop of Derby, Dr A.E.J.Rawlinson.

# Air and Rail

Grass-covered, leafy Brickhill Lane at Burnaston in the summer of 1937. Once it was a coach road. Now it is to be part of an aerodrome. This was the start of Derby Corporation's far-sighted plan for a municipal aerodrome (the word 'airport' was not yet in the dictionary.) The lane crossed the chosen site alongside the road from Derby to Burton. Half a century later it would be the site of the Toyota car factory.

No sooner decided than a start is made. The Mayor of Derby, Alderman Mrs Elizabeth Petty, ceremonially digs into the turf for the start of construction at Burnaston on 29 October 1937.

Not content with doing a spot of digging, Mrs Petty wants to know about the machinery to be used in making the airfield.

A few months later and the levelling of the site is nearly complete. The airfield never had any hard runways, just grass.

The ground is still rather rough but the first plane has landed at Burnaston — 26 April 1938.

The RAF were quick to move in on Burnaston. These huts went up as an RAF Volunteer Reserve training centre was established there in August 1938.

During the summer of 1938 a few privately-owned aircraft were beginning to use Burnaston. When this one arrived carrying six people to the autumn race meeting at Derby, it was hailed as 'the largest aeroplane ever to land at Burnaston'.

Facilities at pre-war Burnaston were not extensive. The Corporation was pleased with how much the aerodrome was being used and this rather hotch-potch wood and canvas hangar was put up speedily in March 1939 to accommodate six more aircraft. It was emphasised that this was just for temporary use.

The official opening of Burnaston Aerodrome was by Air Minister Sir Kingsley Wood in June 1939. Less than three months later, the war started and the RAF took over, making Burnaston an elementary flying training school, a place where many future pilots received their first lessons, amongst them Middlesex and England cricketer Bill Edrich, who was later awarded the DFC. This group was pictured there in 1941.

After the war Burnaston made a fresh start as a civil airfield. In May 1946, an international air taxi service was established there. Mr Frank Kenning, a director of Kenning Aviation Ltd, helps aboard business-women Joyce Lowe, a jeweller, and Teresa Ryan, dress designer, for the inaugural flight to Zurich, with a lunch stop in Paris.

Crowds flocked to Burnaston for an open day and display in June 1947. Skyways flew in their giant airliner, Sky Chieftain — a converted Lancaster bomber.

Derby Aviation came into being and regular services, using converted Dakotas, began from Burnaston. The crew pose by one of them in 1956.

Despite a lack of modern facilities — still only a grass runway — Burnaston stayed free of any serious accidents. There was just the odd mishap, such as this Dakota overshooting in 1963 and having to be towed out of the hayfield.

Burnaston at its peak. This was the layout of facilities as the airport was outgrowing itself in the 1960s. The new East Midlands Airport at Castle Donington, which opened in 1965, was being planned when this picture was taken in 1961.

Derby had its first railway station in 1840. There were rebuildings in 1872 with various additions and changes over the years. This was the Midland Station frontage in the 1920s, just before the regrouping of railway companies that brought the end of the Midland Railway and the formation of the LMS, the London, Midland and Scottish. The inside of the station was rebuilt in the 1950s, but this is how the frontage looked, with minor alterations and some demolitions to the left, until entirely rebuilt in the 1980s.

This was LMS road transport of the 1930s, lined up for inspection at St Mary's Goods Depot in Derby. On the left are some of the mechanical horse-units for towing trailers. Note that some of the drivers still wear leggings as they did for horse-drawn vehicles.

A replica of a locomotive of the past on display among the latest in steam traction at the Derby Loco Works open day, probably at the end of the 1930s. In their heyday of the 1950s, the open days drew tens of thousands of visitors from all over the country.

Open to the sky — but not as planned. This was the Midland Station after it lost its roof in wartime bombing. It provides a view through to the famous Round House of the Loco Works. The inside of the station was rebuilt in the early 1950s.

The lost station. This was Derby Friar Gate on the old Great Northern line, seen here during its declining use in the 1950s. It closed a few years later, falling into dereliction and becoming a wasteland. All that remains is Handyside's ornate bridge over Friar Gate at the end of the station. The bridge itself was under threat in the 1970s but is now preserved as a Victorian feature of a Georgian street.

Dawn of the diesel age. A great moment at Derby Loco Works on 8 December 1947. Emerging from the Diesel Shop is No 10,000 LMS Main Line Diesel Electric Locomotive — the first one built in Britain. At the controls is the Chief Mechanical Engineer of the LMS, Mr H.G.Ivatt.

Survival of steam. Diesel was on the way in but they were still building steam locomotives in Derby. This British Rail Standard Class 5 is seen new out of the Derby works in 1956.

End of the steam age. It is 20 September 1963 and the last steam locomotive to be repaired at the Derby works is given a civic send-off by the Mayor of Derby, Mrs Elsie Mack. The locomotive, a Class 4, had been in service since 1951; it did not have many more years before it.

Steam was out but British Rail research was very much in. There had been an LMS research installation at Derby since 1935 but the big move came in 1961 with the announcement of a major rail engineering laboratory to be built at Derby. This was the start of the British Rail Research Division based in the Railway Technical Centre built on land previously occupied by sidings. Testing equipment still seems rather makeshift in this picture of work at the centre in May 1964, on the day before its official opening by the Duke of Edinburgh.

Derby Station in July 1969 — no trains, no passengers but a lot of work going on. The station closed for 32 hours — longest closure in its history — for the big switchover from semaphore signalling to the new power signalling system, another big advance in railway operation.

The dream that became a nightmare. Research for the APT, the Advanced Passenger Train, began even before the establishment of the Railway Technical Centre but it was there that development was centred in the late 1960s to perfect the 150mph train with a tilt for going around bends. This was the laboratory built at the centre for testing the APT.

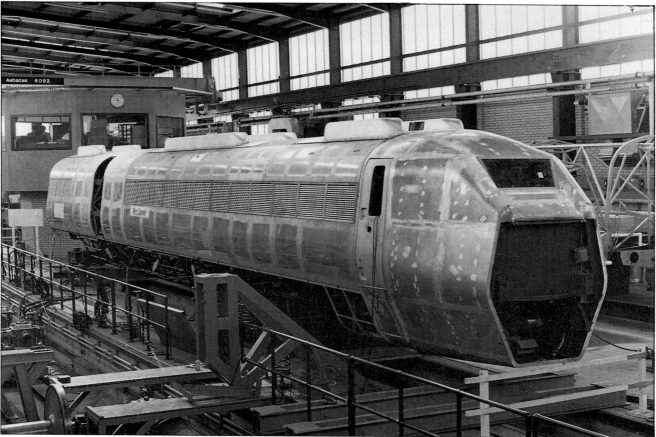

The first APT power car takes shape alongside the roller test rig in the advanced projects laboratory.

The old station as it will be remembered. This was about ten years before its 1985 rebuilding. Compare it with the 1920s picture to spot the few changes in 50 years. The clock with its wyvern, symbol of the Midland Railway, is preserved in the station car park.

The prototype advanced train getting to an advanced stage of testing. The body shells were made by Metro-Cammell at Birmingham and brought by road to the Derby laboratory; the bogies were assembled at the Derby Loco Works.

The first appearance of the APT, moving from the Railway Technical Centre into Derby Station. It is 25 July 1972 — beyond the time scale covered by this collection of pictures. The rest of the sad tale of the APT was told through the 1970s and into the 1980s before an end was put to the whole project and the three prototypes.

# Weathering It All

Although the winter of 1947 has lived on in the national memory as the worst of the century, that of 1940 was as bad, if not worse, in Derby as these scenes show. Cleared snow is piled at the roadsides in the Market Place but more has fallen to cover the roads again.

The Warwick Avenue section of Derby ring-road in January 1940. It seems that they are using lorries and dustcarts to move snow and dump it in the central reservation. Even pictures like this were subject to the censor's approval in that first winter of the war.

Soldiers of the Sherwood Foresters from Normanton Barracks help out with the snow-clearing at Allestree.

Delivering the milk by sledge. That seems to be the case. In 1940 some local farmers had their own milk rounds with horse-drawn floats and, when the snow blocked the roads, other means of getting the milk out had to be found.

The bitter winter of 1940 was followed by a glorious summer and a good crop of blackberries. These boys at Breadsall are out collecting the free supplement to wartime food supplies.

Another summer, another scene — and one that is unrecognisable now. This is the edge of Markeaton Park; behind the fence is Kedleston Road and in years to come the college buildings of Derby University will rise high on the hill in the background.

The rains came — 3.25 inches in 36 hours. Culverted Markeaton Brook could not take the flow. And the centre of Derby was flooded — up to 8ft deep. This was Sunday, 22 May 1932. The water rose during the night and by dawn it was above the marker plates on walls showing the depth of the 1842 flood. Then it receded as quickly as it came. Here are scenes in the Wardwick; Cornmarket looking towards the Market Place; Cornmarket towards Victoria Street, where workmen are clearing drains; and boating down St James's Street.

The water soon flowed from the streets but cellars were still flooded and destruction was left behind. Sightseers step over cleared out rubble and workmen operate a hand pump to get the water out of a shop cellar in St James's Street.

Salvaging soaked council documents from the flooded basement of the Town Hall. The Mayor, Alderman William Salisbury (third from the left), quickly launched a relief fund — damage along the line of the flood from the West End to the Derwent was put at £400,000, more than £20-million in today's terms. Hanging up council papers to dry is Denis Gilman, then assistant solicitor with Derby Corporation, later Clerk of Derbyshire County Council, the top county post.

Printing presses and rolls of newsprint in the flooded basement of Northcliffe House in Albert Street, home of *Derby Evening Telegraph*. Editions of the newspapers, telling the story of the great flood, had to be printed at Leicester.

The reason for the flood was that the culvert taking Markeaton Brook under the town could not cope with the amount of water. The brook had been an open sewer through the centre of the town — hence the name, the Strand — until culverting began in the 1830s, first with the Victoria Street length. This picture, taken inside the culvert after the 1932 flood, shows some of the revetting that was there when the brook was open.

Strengthening of the culvert was done in 1939, as seen in this view from under the Strand, looking towards the buried Sadler Gate Bridge, built in 1787 to replace two medieval bridges.

The culvert was extensively reconstructed in 1967. This view from the Strand shows the demolition of that central wall seen in the 1939 picture. Beyond are the trees of Boden's Pleasance; the culvert was rebuilt under there and Bold Lane car park was built on top of it.

More strengthening of the culvert was done along Victoria Street in 1957.

The improved culvert removed the danger of town centre flooding but Little Chester area was still vulnerable to flooding from the Derwent. This was Old Chester Road when the river overflowed in December 1965.

Lorries try their luck and come to grief along Mansfield Road during the 1965 flood. An extensive flood protection scheme was put in hand after this.

Exeter Bridge can just take it. This was the maximum height reached by the Derwent in 1965.

Out of town, the worst flooding incident happened in 1947 when the foundations of the old Cavendish Bridge over the Trent at Shardlow were undermined and the bridge collapsed.

It took just over ten years to build the new bridge at Shardlow. In those days before motorways, the A6 was the main road to London and this wartime-design Bailey bridge, with one-way traffic, had to cope for all those years.

The Bailey bridge in the foreground and the new bridge beyond, nearing completion.

# Fire and Destruction

The day after the 1932 great flood, came the great explosion. Gas escaping from a main damaged by the flood filled the cellar of Samuel's the jewellers, in Cornmarket. At two o'clock that Monday afternoon, 23 May 1932, with crowds thronging the street, it exploded. Ten people were injured. Police are here seen leading the salvage operation. Jewellery, clocks and watches were scattered over the pavement and road. The area was cordoned off and every shovelful of debris gathered up was sifted to find any jewels or fragments of precious metal.

Derby had its own fire brigade from shortly after becoming a county borough in the 1880s until reorganisation after World War Two put it to an increasing extent under the control of the county. These were some of Derby's firemen — but not in these uniforms and with this equipment. They are recreating firefighting of the past for the 1954 pageant that celebrated the octocentenary of Derby's first charter.

Derby Fire Station and the brigade headquarters was in Bold Lane. Here, in 1948 when the brigade was at its diamond jubilee, the fire engines are on parade for inspection. The fire station was demolished in 1963 — and later Bold Lane multi-storey car park was built there.

During the war years fire brigades amalgamated into the National Fire Service, with the military-style steel helmet replacing the traditional fireman's helmet. Here NFS men fight a 1943 fire in the stand at Derby Racecourse.

The vast expanses of railway works at Derby were always particular fire risks. This was the damage done in one fire soon after nationalisation. Worse was to come to the Carriage and Wagon Works later in the 1950s.

One of their last big fires fought as the NFS. This blaze at a factory in Siddals Road was in October 1947, shortly before the fire
service reverted to regional organisation.

In the early hours of Wednesday, 28 March 1956 fire swept through Derby Playhouse, the repertory theatre in Sacheverel Street, opened four years before. The flames left the auditorium a mere shell. Here are views of the stage, open to the sky, and the remains of some of the auditorium seating.

Actress Ann Kennedy surveys the Playhouse damage. She was appearing in the new play being staged that week. There had been just two performances of it. Its fate-tempting title was *The Wick and the Wax* and the play in rehearsal for staging the following week was called *High Temperature*.

We'll rise again, promised the Playhouse. Little more than a year after the fire, it was back in business. This was the stage set for *My Three Angels*, the production for the reopening on 25 April 1957. The theatre then adopted the Phoenix, rising from the flames, as its symbol, replaced by the Eagle when the new Derby Playhouse opened in the Eagle Centre complex in 1975.

Twice in the space of a year, fires ravaged the Derby Carriage and Wagon Works of British Railways. This was some of the devastation caused by the first one in 1957.

This dramatic picture was taken at the height of the second blaze at the Carriage and Wagon Works, the following September.

The building gone, the twisted metal of carriages remaining after the 1958 fire at the Carriage and Wagon Works.

The hole in the roof. At first it was thought that the fire at Derby's 18th-century Assembly Rooms on 15 February 1963 had not done damage that was too severe. The fire was confined to the roof of the building where the town's gentry had met, danced and been seen for 200 years. In fact the blaze had weakened the entire structure and the Assembly Rooms could not be saved.

Firemen clearing up after the the 1963 blaze at the Assembly Rooms.

Supported by scaffolding, the derelict Assembly Rooms stood for the rest of the decade. The line of buildings on the left of the picture, together with the original site, is where the new Assembly Rooms would be built at the end of the 1970s.

DEMOLITION
THIS CAR PARK WILL BE

When what remained of the old Assembly Rooms was eventually demolished in 1971, the façade was taken down stone by stone and two years later was re-erected as part of the old street scene in the National Tramways Museum at Crich.

# Sporting Scene

The start of the 1930 cricket season and, led by their skipper, Captain Guy Jackson, Derbyshire take the field against Sussex at the County Ground. The date on the pavilion behind them is 1884 but this had been the home of the county club since its formation in 1870.

Out of whites and into a wide variety of clothing styles. These were some of the Derbyshire 1st XI of 1931.

Although Burton upon Trent is in Staffordshire, Derbyshire have played there, at various grounds, on and off throughout their history. This is the 1935 side, captained by Arthur Richardson, making Derbyshire's first visit to Burton for five years. This was the team which finished second in the County Championship in 1935 and went on to take the county title the following year. Derbyshire have not won the Championship since.

Derbyshire CCC in 1935. Back row (left to right): A.E.Alderman, T.B.Mitchell, D.Smith, A.V.Pope, G.H.Pope, T.S.Worthington, E.Carrington. Front row: H.Storer, H.Elliott, A.W.Richardson (captain), H.Parker (honorary scorer), L.F.Townsend. Albert Alderman and Harry Storer also played soccer for Derby County, Storer later managing the Rams. Arthur Richardson's son and grandson have both played for the County, and Tommy Mitchell, who went on the infamous England 'Bodyline' tour to Australia in the 1930s, was still alive in 1993, aged 91.

This is how the County Ground looked in that Championship season of 1936 — minus the crowds for this is only a practice match. The adjoining racecourse was still very much in use. Although the grandstand seen in this picture is still a familiar sight in the 1990s, the cricket ground of the 1930s was separated from that stand by the racecourse itself. The last race meeting was in August 1939. In the background to the right are the stables and other buildings which were demolished for housing development in the late 1950s.

Honour for the champions — and special honour for two of them, Bill Copson and, having his hand shaken by skipper Arthur Richardson, Stanley Worthington. Supporters and fellow members of the team are seeing the pair off at Derby Midland Station on their way to join the England party for the 1936-37 tour of Australia.

Two years later, with several members of the Championship side still there but there is a new captain, Robin Buckston (right) to lead out Derbyshire.

Back in the cricketing business after the war. And Stan Worthington, from that 1936 Championship side, is still scoring the runs. Here at the start of the 1946 season he returns to the pavilion 147 not out at the end of Derbyshire's innings against Leicestershire.

Others from the Championship side are still there in this 1947 picture — Bill Copson, Albert Alderman and Denis Smith. 'New Boy', on the right, is A.E.G. 'Dusty' Rhodes who played his first match in 1937. He continued to play into the 1950s when his son, Harold, also joined Derbyshire.

A new stand at the County Ground, to the right of the pavilion, for the 1939 season. It didn't look very impressive then. In a derelict state, it was still there nearly half a century later.

A packed ground in July 1948 for the visit of the Australians to Derby. The view is from the racecourse grandstand but racing ended nine years before. The course ran across the foreground where the marquee and cars are. The stand built in 1939 is beyond the pavilion on the right.

Many at that 1948 Australians' match came to see Don Bradman, but Derbyshire skipper Eddie Gothard bowled him first ball.

Derbyshire CCC in 1952. Back row (left to right): J.M.Kelly, A.Hamer, G.O.Dawkes, H.L.Jackson, D.C.Morgan, A.C.Revill, E.Smith, A.Hobson (masseur). Front row: A.E.G.Rhodes, D.B.Carr, G.L.Willatt (captain), C.S.Elliott, C.Gladwin. Donald Carr later became secretary of Derbyshire CCC and then of the TCCB. Charlie Elliott and 'Dusty' Rhodes were both Test Match umpires.

Down it comes. With the playing area to be moved over nearer to the Grandstand and a new batting square to be laid, the old pavilion is demolished at the end of the 1954 season.

The start of the 1955 season and the opening of the new ground layout, with the Grandstand brought into use and the old race judges' stand and offices adapted into a pavilion. This is how it continued until the building of the Lund Pavilion in the 1980s, although the Grandstand is still a major feature of the ground and Derbyshire hope to purchase it.

Whatever became of this idea? It is 1954 at Rolls-Royce Welfare Sports Ground where they are experimenting with the possibility of using a Derwent jet engine to dry out a cricket pitch after rain . . .!

Derby County Football Club grew out of Derbyshire County Cricket Club. It was formed in 1884 to raise extra revenue for the hard-up cricketers. The Rams played first at the County Ground, were founder members of the Football League in 1888 and moved to the Baseball Ground in 1895. The first time they dropped to the Second Division was in 1907 and they had been up and down twice before this team picture was taken in March 1933. They had been back in the First Division since 1926 and would stay until 1953. In this line-up are (back row, left to right): Tommy Cooper, Ralph Hann (later the Rams' trainer), Jack Nicholas ('Owd Nick', later chief scout), Jack Kirby, Louis Edwards (trainer), George Collin, Jack Barker (manager from 1953 to 1955) and Ike Keen; (front row): Sammy Crooks (later chief scout), Duncan Hutchison, Jack Bowers (later assistant trainer), Peter Ramage and Douglas 'Dally' Duncan.

In the 1930s, the *Derby Evening Telegraph* ran a weekly cartoon about that week's doings at the Baseball Ground. This one celebrates two great Rams players, Jack Barker and Jack Bowers, both of whom joined the club from Midland League football after being spotted in opposition in the same game.

A great Derby County player — perhaps the greatest — Steve Bloomer, then a general assistant at the Baseball Ground, has a captive
audience of, from left to right, Syd Wileman, Sammy Crooks, Dally Duncan, Jack Nicholas, Jack Barker and Jack Bowers.

Mourning the King. Before their match at the Baseball Ground, Derby County and Nottingham Forest players line up to observe silence on the death of King George V in January 1936.

No, it's not the Rams training at the Baseball Ground but members of the Home Guard, limbering up with a spot of PE. Note the bomb-damaged Osmaston Stand, which was hit in January 1941, during Derby's worst air-raid of the war.

The day they won the FA Cup. It is 27 April 1946 and Derby County are at Wembley for the first time. They had been in three previous Cup Finals — before Wembley was built — and had lost all, the last one 6-0 to Bury in 1903. Now in this first Cup Final after the war they met Charlton Athletic. Before the toss (which Charlton won), Derby captain Jack Nicholas shakes hands with opposing skipper Don Welsh, watched by referee Mr E.D.Smith (Whitehaven).

It's four to one. Four Charlton defenders, but inside-left Peter Doherty is the only Derby player in sight as goalkeeper Sam Bartram punches the ball away. But it was 4-1 the other way in the match's final score, Derby scoring three goals in extra time after the first 80 minutes had been goalless.

Home with the Cup. It is still the only time that it has been possible to take a picture of the Rams with the FA Cup. Back row (left to right): Jack Parr, Jim Bullions, Jack Nicholas, Vic Woodley, Jack Howe, Leon Leuty and Chick Musson. Middle row: Sammy Crooks, Jack Stamps, Stuart McMillan (manager), directors T.A.Wassell, B.Robshaw (chairman), H.Walker and J.R.Cholerton, Peter Doherty, Raich Carter and trainer Dave Willis. In front are Reg Harrison and Dally Duncan.

Tommy Powell, who played over 400 games for the Rams and whose son, Steve, also gave the club magnificent service, in action during a Third Division North game against great rivals Grimsby Town. The Derby player to the left is Eire international and Rams skipper Reg Ryan. Those Third North days were great fun, the Rams scoring well over 200 goals in their two seasons in that division with attendances often topping 30,000. Tommy Powell later worked in the *Evening Telegraph's* accounts department for many years.

Another decade, another division. This was the Derby first-team squad in the Second Division at the start of the 1960-61 season — which whey finished in 12th place. Back row are (left to right): Brian Daykin, Frank Upton, Geoff Barrowcliffe, Ken Oxford, Ray Young, Mike Smith and Glyn Davies. Middle row, Barry Hutchinson, Paddy Fagan, Jack Parry, Peter Thompson, George Darwin and Dave Cargill. In front, Tommy Powell (whose son, Steve, followed him to the Baseball Ground in 1971) and Tony Conwell.

The coming of Clough. It was in July 1967 that Brian Clough, with assistant Peter Taylor, became Derby County manager. He was to stay for six years that were flowing with success on the field and topped up with turbulence off it. He took the Rams back into the First Division in his second season and to the Football League championship in 1971-72 (for the first time in the club's history), reaching the European Cup semi-finals the following year. Newcomers Taylor and Clough are here pictured with club chairman (and future adversary) Sam Longson and former Sunderland star Len Shackleton, on whose recommendation they came from Hartlepools United.

At last another trophy. Skipper Dave Mackay holds aloft the Second Division championship cup after the highly successful 1968-69 season. Mackay was the man Clough brought in to provide the experience and inspiration in the young new team he was building. Mackay was to return to Derby as manager after Clough, from 1973 to 1976, during which Derby again won the First Division title.

Members of the 1969 team stand on the steps of Derby Council House, with the Second Division championship trophy, before going in for a civic reception.

Inside the Council House, manager Brian Clough is received by the Mayor, Councillor Mrs Edith Wood.

More Rams celebrations and a civic reception came when they went one better to win the League championship in 1972. Here they make their triumphant progress through the town centre with both the championship trophy and the Texaco Cup, for which they beat Airdrieonians in the Final. It was competed for by English and Scottish clubs.

A band was playing outside the Council House to greet the triumphant players.

Derby Parks Department responded to the Rams' success with this carpet-bedding floral salute in Darley Park.

Boardroom battles and enmity off the pitch finally bubbled over. Brian Clough and Peter Taylor went in October 1973. And they stayed gone despite a vigorous campaign to bring them back. This was part of a protest march through the centre of Derby. It was the end of an era.

# BOXING

## KING'S HALL, DERBY
## MONDAY, FEBRUARY 8th, 1960

Commence **7.30** p.m.        Doors open **6.45** p.m.

A

# Joe Woodhouse

## PROMOTION

# PROGRAMME 6d.

ALVASTON PRESS, DERBY

Up to the 1960s there were several thousand licensed professional boxers in the UK and most towns and cities featured regular shows. Before the war there was professional boxing in Derby at the Drill Hall and the Municipal Sports Stadium. Afterwards, fortnightly shows were held at the King's Hall (actually Queen Street Baths and now the refurbished Queen's Leisure Centre).

The journey through the years, looking at changing Derby during the middle section of the 20th century, is complete. Quietly rowing away on Derby's river is this 1957 crew of Derwent Rowing Club, founded in 1857, just a hundred years before.

# Bibliography

Body, G. *Railway Stations of Britain*, Wellingborough, 1990.
Craven, M. *Derby: An Illustrated History*. Derby, 1988.
Craven, M. *Images of Derby 1860-1960*. Derby, 1990.
Craven, M. (editor) *Winter's Collection of Derby*. Derby, 1992.
Glover, S. *Glover's Derby*. Derby, 1843.
Greatrex, H.N. *Melville's Derby Legacy*. Derby, 1985.
Hammerton, G. *Front Page News*. Derby, 1989.
Hardy C. & Brown R. *Derby at War*. Birmingham, 1979.
Marsden, C.J. *25 Years of Railway Research*. Yeovil, 1989.
Mortimer, G. *Derby County: A Complete Record*. Derby, 1988.
Richardson, W.A. *Citizen's Derby*. London, 1949.
Rippon, Anton. *The Book of Derby*. Derby, 1993.
Wilson, H.S. *History of Post in Derby*. London, 1990.
*Derby Evening Telegraph*, newspaper issues, 1920-1970.
*Derbyshire County Cricket Year Book*, various years.

# SUBSCRIBERS

## PRESENTATION COPY
The Mayor of Derby

1 Geoff Hammerton
2 S Anderson-Dixon Esq
3 M Lowe Esq
4 Anton Rippon
5 John Grainger
6 Graham Hales
7 Ian Potter
8 Mick Derby
9 Kathleen Holt
10 Mr & Mrs F C Ward
11 Adrian Wildbore
12 Robert Webb
13 Andrew L & Susan Fletcher
14 Pat Wildgoose
15 Karon Fox
16 M J F Newton
17 Alan Watson
18 Mr & Mrs H A Stone
19 Roy Siviter
20 Stephen Hanson
21 R E Spooner
22 L W & V M Gregory
23 Raymond Anthony Beck
24 Edward J Bland
25 Cora Ratcliffe
26 Arthur H Sowter
27 William C Burton
28 Mrs Florence A Paxton
29 R D Rhodes
30 Dorothy Watson
31 John Gates
32 Michael Allgood
33 A Chapman
34 John Moxhay
35 Percy L Davis
36 Stephen Higgins
37 N M & E R Pickford
38 G J Greatorex
39 Audrey & George Harlow
40 Sheila Harrison
41 John P Cook
42 Mr Kenneth Chatterley
43 Mr Steven May
44 Paul Shimmin
45 A R Wheatley
46 John Fletcher
47 Allan William Burgoyne
48 Phyllis & Martin Du Sautoy

49 Albert Maurice Smith
50 Ken Taylor
51 Anthony Michael Johnson
52 David A Walker
53 J Roberts
54 Kate Ireland
55 Mr A Lee
56 Mr K R Rodgers
57 W W Bromley
58 John Arthur Hedley Snr
59 Alan Hunt
60 George Selwood
61 Leslie Campbell
62 Mr Adrian Lunn
63 J Mathers
64 Doreen M Cox
65 Mr Leslie Halford
66 Mrs S Lawn
67 Norman Ingman
68 John A Harvey
69 Mrs M Kingman
70 Mr H J Wallis
71 A J Drury
72 Alan Richards
73 Royal Banqueting Suite
74 Patricia A Jackson
75 Donald Anthony Eyden
76 D C Midgley
77 D M Hawksworth
78 Frank Burton
79 Michael Wileman
80 Alan Boiling
81 R S Brindley
82 Kathleen Bailey
83 Derek & Maisie Fisher
84 William Murray
85 Raymond Tudor
86 Mrs M A Jones
87 R B Abell
88 James R Freeman
89 B N & I P Leuty
90 Joan Lowis
91 Jean M Evans
92 Dorothy E Hawley
93 Michael Thomas Arnott
94 Mr & Mrs P Vasbund
95 Nicola Crowther
96 G H Woodings
97 F M Rivett
98 Michael R Bratby

99 Graham J Moore
100 Maurice Murfin
101 Mr Chris Drury
102 Michael & Anne Smith
103 Peter Kite
104 Keith Whittingham
105 E J Webster
106 Mrs P Barteczko
107 R A & B Stone
108 A E Knight
109 J & S W Redfern
110 Fredrick Paul & Sharon Zita Milwain
111 John F Morrell
112 Mike & Hazel Barraclough
113 Mrs Mandy Jane Harris
114 Grandad Betts
115 Thomas & Dorothy Lloyd
116 Mr K C Saunders
117 David & Linda Stanier
118 David W Slater
119 J K Windle
120 Mrs Dorothy Walton
121 Rita Thompson
122 Kenneth Francis Woodward
123 E B Blackshaw
124 J C Seaman
125 D S Marsden
126 Mr T A Parsons
127 Eileen Wright
128 Mrs Marjorie Williams
129 Roy S Swinson
130 Janet Mitchell
131 Wendy Urwin
132 Tim Lipscomb
133 Mary A Knight
134 Brian Renshaw
135 Charlotte Marie Bullock
136 Mr D P Harris
137 Joy O P Taylor
138 A L Wild
139 Brian Eric Reedman
140 Brian Fearn
141 A J Brown
142 Henniker
143 Mr D J Jakeman
144 G M Shaw
145 C W Hurd
146 Mrs Marguerite Faulkner

147 Fred & Fay Luscombe
148 William-Beckett Jnr
149 Miss P R Bown
150 Miss E J Shepherd
151 Harry & Dorothy Fisher
152 Donald & Annette Ashfield
       (Toronto, Canada)
153 Jean & Graham Mabbitt
154 Wayne & Rebecca Pettifer
155 Doreen M Hanson
156 Mr & Mrs C W Hall
157 R Needham
158 Lynne & Steve Gibbons
159 Patricia A Jackson
160 Vilma Ann Barton
161 M J & S R Coates
162 Colin Paulin
163 Eric A Swales
164 Harold S Wilson
165 D H Woolliscroft
166 John Wass
167 Frank Wright
168 Gill & Alan Hiley
169 Brenda Williams
170 Desmond Parkinson
171 Alan & Margaret Sitdown
172 Mr & Mrs R Shaw
173 S M Leahy
174 Mrs J Brookes
175 Mrs Mary Golding
176 Karl Bucknall
177 Mike & Sue Radford
178 William Edward Blount
179 Nigel J Tilly
180 Pauline Tanner
181 Donald Simmons
182 D M Higginbottom
183 Albert Edward Watson
184 Mrs E Askey
185 John Render
186 Patricia E Eland
187 Doris Simpson
188 Mary Gayda
189 Alan David Webster
190 Brian & Margaret Blissett
191 Philip Singleton
192 Mrs R Stubley
193 P C & F E Barlow
194 Mr L H Fowkes
195 R A H O'Neal
196 Stanley Evans
197 Mrs M C Dyson
198 Mr H Patrick
199 A Loadman
200 Mrs M E Lloyd
201 Michael E Briggs
202 John M Naden
203 David A Naden

204 Paul Hilsdon
205 A W Garton
206 Derek G Hill
207 Mrs Doris Middleton
208 Anthony Sewter
209 June Lord
210 Colin & Patricia Meynell
211 William Henderson
212 Mrs J D Hassall
213 M Ainsworth
214 Richard Attwood
215 Mr Derek Osman
216 Brian D Casterton
217 Miss J M Fletcher
218 P R & C J Rhodes
219 Graham W Glynn
220 Mr R Neal
221 F Spendlove
222 Salloway & Associates
223 J E & J R Moon
224 Vera Hurford
225 Mr & Mrs J McLean
226 P A Cripwell
227 Jeanne Bordekin
228 Mrs Vera Henderson
229 Mrs June Henson
230 A J Emerton
231 Betty Henderson
232 T C Ford
233 Bill Heseltine
234 Mrs E V Cooper
235 P Baker
236 A H Sherwood
237 Doreen & Gordon Bethell
238 S J Dunning
239 Peter & Jane Ratcliff
240 Trevor & Rosalie Ratcliff
241 David A Brough
242 Janet E Howells
243 C K Lee
244 Christopher Shelton
245 R D Burley
246 B R & D Farnsworth
247 H C Coleman
248 John & Allen Painter
249 Mr Paul Craven
250 Sydney Chell
251 Eric Stanhope
252 Mr T A Parsons
253 P Purnell
254 A C Edmonds
255 A J Worrall
256 Mrs M Bancroft
257 Ron Williams
258 J I Hall
259 Mark R Crawford
260 Peter Kirkman
261 John S R Borsley

262 Anthony John Casterton
263 Chris & Stuart Weightman
264 Marc A Whittaker
265 A Norton
266 T O Topham
267 J M Nottingham
268 Don Gardner
269 W A Whitbread
270 Dorothy Arnold
271 Audrey Eileen Boiling
272 Steve & Melanie Fowkes
273 Peter T King
274 Mrs J H Taylor
275 Norman Beardsley
276 F & K M Burridge
277 Mr Barry Smith
278 D W Parkin
279 Mr Brian Newberry
280 Miss J M Hallsworth
281 Vic S Wright
282 Peter E Dawson
283 Mr F Winfield
284 B R Hallett
285 Herbert Allen
286 Mr L Kilbourne
287 Mr & Mrs B Fearn
288 Brian Knight
289 Mr John Calladine
290 Ernest Howarth
291 Winifred May Owen
292 John Dutton
293 S M Kelly
294 Mr B J Evans
295 Mr Michael Clubb
296 John R Chambers
297 D Martin
298 T E & P Gibbons
299 Stan Smith
300 Miss Melanie Yates
301 Joan & Alf Milner
302 Howard Bettany
303 William Fletcher
304 Bernard E Brown
305 F C Foster
306 M Clamp
307 P A Samways
308 Mr E W & Mrs K Selfe
309 H W Richardson
310 Mrs J L Lings
311 Mr Michael R Pegg
312 Barry Carrington
313 J E W Holland
314 S J Holland
315 Anna & James Beeson
316 Ronald Birks
317 Mrs Fruse Jones
318 Antony Paul Redfern
319 Maurice Edward Beardmore

320 Muriel Sellors
321 Mr Donald Kenneth Hubbard
322 Keith John Siddons
323 Mr F W Odell
324 Rob K Eaglesfield
325 Ken Wright
326 F G Ford Slater
327 Brenda Bunting
328 D W & M M Walton
329 Mrs J M Easter
330 J K Braidley
331 Percival Maurice Wilton
332 Maurice Jordan
333 Mr G G Wells
334 Sheila Wheatley
335 Owen Worthy
336 Mr Alex Anderson
337 Alan G Foster
338 Jean Phipps
339 P J Woolley
340 John Richard Beardmore
341 Barbara Field Dunton
342 Cyril Ross
343 Paul B Ross
344 M A Green
345 Mr H F Harris
346 Margaret R Mack
347 Kathleen M Leigh
348 John & Hazel Smith
349 Mrs Marilyn C Gilbert
350 Susan Giles
351 Mr Alan Warburton
352 Mr John Robert Stubbs
353 Sam Harrison
354 W H & J R Wood
355 R Gale
356 Margaret Wilmot
357 Kenneth Brewin
358 Victor Dorrington
359 Mrs J M Eason
360 Hubert J Jarvis
361 Mrs Beryl Hopkinson
362 H R Williamson
363 Barbara A Douglas
364 Mrs Anne Haslam
365 Vivienne Leigh
366 Catherine & Stanley Hardy
367 Mr S Weston
368 Alan Milward
369 Mrs M A Dolman
370 R G Lomas
371 Arthur James Key
372 Flora Kibbler
373 Marilyn Gillings
374 A H Blood
375 Marilyn F Hutton
376 Roger W Jerram

377 William Harvey Baker
378 Mrs B A Richardson
379 Mark Harvey
380 Bill Holmes
381 Sandra I Wharton
382 Des Hartshorn
383 Hilda Kent
384 Christopher Cohen
385 Michael Cohen
386 Gordon Sidney Waite
387 Marie Rowley
388 Mr & Mrs D K Pollard
389 Mrs O M Murfin
390 Mrs M A Oddie
391 Nicholas Harpur
392 G I M Ruddle
393 John L Skidmore
394 Barbara Edwards
395 Victor Oscroft
396 Brian Freeman
397 Stephen Darby
398 Mr & Mrs W Calladine
399 Mr & Mrs Mellor
400 Terence Bagnall
401 Mr B Hazlewood
402 Mr & Mrs L D Brown
403 Mr D Dodd
404 J W & D E Hammond
405 G & R Warner
406 K & I Warner
407 E C White FCA
408 E C White FCA
409 Ivor Grace
410 F E Thurgood
411 Mr E R Neville
412 Joan & Gordon Tunnicliff
413 Nadene Shrigley
414 Charles P Harrison
415 L Lloyd
416 David Henry Worthington
417 Leonard Matthews
418 S J Barker
419 Paul Stewart Johnson
420 Ivy Cook
421 Dr & Mrs A R Clayton
422 S E Martin
423 Kevin G W Litting
424 Marcus E W Litting
425 Mr H N Lawrence
426 Mrs M Tomlinson
427 D M Learman
428 Mr L Broughton
429 Fay M Stevenson
430 David Russell Long
431 Mrs J Rawson
432 Patricia V Boa
433 Patricia V Boa
434 M E Robson

435 Christine Hague
436 L G Lofting
437 R E Mays
438 Jack Rudd
439 Tony William Sharratt
440 Betty Morgan
441 Mr Derek Kirkman
442 Maureen C Webb
443 Mrs A J Wood
444 Mr R D Brett
445 Mrs J Clark
446 Colin & Judith Fitzhugh
447 Mr Peter Oakden
448 Joyce M Ramsden
449 Richard M Collins
450 Victor Arthur Handley
451 Barbara A Bryant
452 M Dunlop
453 Arthur Wagstaff
454 Roy Jackson
455 Mr Colin Peter Wood
456 Jean Waters
457 D J Stirland
458 Mr Jack Staton
459 D W Bradley
460 Graham Hall
461 Philip Thomas
462 David Parry
463 Ian Griffiths
464 John L Harley
465 Alan Cooper
466 T J Larimore
467 R M Larimore
468 Mrs Joyce V King
469 Miss B H Rose
470 Jean Storey
471 J P Lissimore
472 Dorothy Clarke
473 Freda N Brooks
474 Eileen M Hopkins
475 Mr & Mrs P D Selvey
476 Glyn Hodgetts
477 Alan Stewart JP
478 Pete Rowbottom
479 Kevin Speakman
480 J R Fletcher
481 Harry & Betty Witnall
482 Allan & Pat Burton
483 Brian D Taylor
484 Richard Andrew Mead
485 Andrew Michael Gaida
486 Carole & Gary Mortimer
487 Dick Bowen
488 Brian Lawrence Edwards
489 N Harrison
490 M E Hudson
491 Mr Dennis Worthington
492 Fred D Fisher

493 Graham Harvey
494 K A Pether
495 Barbara Paddison
496 Barbara Paddison
497 Len Seal
498 B E Shuff
499 Maureen Schafer
500 Frederick G Spencer
501 Marie Nicholson
502 Harry Piggott
503 Betty Graves
504 Pamela Spencer
505 Mr Keith Webb
506 Bernard W Page
507 Sheila & John Taylor
508 Pam Gordon
509 J E Morley
510 C G Fletcher
511 A J Rawson
512 M R Williamson
513 Mr J D Bancroft
514 Len & Linda Murfin
515 Len & Linda Murfin
516 Peter Parkin
517 Gordon Gerald Chattle
518 Mrs D M Dixon
519 Mrs D M Dixon
520 Vida Ayres
521 Harold S Ayres
522 Keith Hassall
523 Pamela Stevens
524 Alkia Dyche
525 Heather Chambers
526 Mr J E Browning
527 Miss C D Todd
528 Pheasant
529 Mary Lawrence
530 R F Stokes
531 Mr M J R Morley
532 Derek Nix
533 Valerie Jean King
534 Tony Radford
535 S Thornhill
536 Ian Gooding
537 Trevor & Beverley Bennett
538 Mrs Iris Stone
539 Peggy & Graham Weston
540 Brenda & John Wilkinson
541 Kevin Eley
542 Dr F K Hammond
543 Keith Broughton
544 Stuart H D Wilkins
545 R J Cook
546 Arthur Eley
547 Kevin M Backler
548 Dorothy & Geoff Smith
549 Mrs R L Padmore
550 D W Goodwill

551 Julia Bath
552 Mr E H Alcock
553 Mrs I Foster
554 Richard H Billinge
555 K I Alderson
556 J W Middleton
557 Mr Peter Joseph Forman
558 A R Wareing
559 Henry J Eyre
560 Clara Elsie Wright
561 Clare J Mogridge
562 T Pe Clarke
563 John L Hobson
564 R S Potter
565 Mrs Pamela Wright
566 Victor Richard Norvaisa
567 Mrs Barbara Henson
568 Walter Spencer Bates
569 Tracey H Brookes
570 J Barwise
571 Bob & Roma Wilcock
572 H F Stewart
573 Colin Scales
574 David Sanders
575 George B Humphries
576 Lewis Rose
577 Mr & Mrs G Henman
578 Mr & Mrs T Powell
579 Peter M Stanley
580 Neville Wild
581 Cherry Holme
582 Bryan Hill
583 C G Smith
584 Noel G King
585 Jean Weaver
586 P R & J Binks
587 Reg & Marjorie Lee
588 Brian G Marson
589 L T Beeston
590 B E Cash
591 Jeremy David Tye
592 David Wheeldon
593 Harold F Sharp (Australia)
594 Hilda Day
595 John F King
596 May Stanhope
597 K M Hammond
598 Kenneth Ward
599 Mrs Kathleen Elizabeth
      Fordham
600 Margaret Midgley
601 Mr Cyril Goddard
602 F & S A Duerden
603 A F Bushby
604 Mr Albert Edward Meakin
605 Elizabeth H Porter
606 Mr A J F Drayton
607 Mr J F Drayton

608 Hazelle Bruce-Ewen
609 B A Reid
610 L W Lamb
611 R Lamb
612 Ron F Williamson
613 Mr & Mrs V J Barber
614 V A Ward
615 Ian & June Fletcher
616 Norma Consterdine
617 Joyce Poynton
618 L F Brown
619 E M Stephenson
620 Mr A G Dowdy
621 Peter McMahon
622 Doug Smith
623 B A Lacey
624 Elizabeth Eisenberg
625 Mrs D Johnson
626 Granville Pessoll
627 Mike McLoughlin
628 David J Bagley
629 Mr William James
      Holland
630 K H Daniels
631 Brian Tye
632 Pam & John Donnelly
633 Wendy R L Gilmore
634 Stephen Edwards
635 Roy & Linda Young
636 G Kathleen Pearson
637 Mr D A Church
638 Phil Rogers
639 Richard G Hodgkinson
640 Brian H Woodall
641 Steven Mann
642 Judith Ann Robinson
643 Peter Mason
644 Doris Bickerdike
645 Norman Fielding
646 Shirley Pywell
647 Blossom Barbara Utal
648 Yvonne Whilton
649 Joseph Mason
650 Derick A Perry
651 David J Crampton
652 Mike & Joice Kelley
653 Brian Goodwin
654 Mrs M Blood
655 Mrs M Blood
656 Mrs June Lawrence
657 Margaret & Frank Elliott
658 Doreen & Ronald
      Thompson (USA)
659 Patricia M Smith
660 Marjorie Nina Simpson
661 L Wilson
662 Mr L K North
663 Stephen Wilshaw

664 Ian David Rogers
665 W H T Dukes
666 Elaine Oakley & Stuart Brunyee
667 Margaret & Laurence McLoughlin
668 N Broadhead
669 Arthur Pickles
670 John Huddlestone
671 Mr B E Wilson
672 Gillian Ludlam
673 Roy F Brownsword
674 D R Hall
675 Clifford McLoughlin
676 Barrie & Wendy Dunn
677 Ian Ludlam
678 D P Jones
679 Sheila Hadfield
680 N D Merritt
681 Mrs Susan Pinchbeck
682 Albert Edward Dalton
683 D G Buckler
684 Philp Fletcher
685 Philp Fletcher
686 Barry Hardy
687 Gladys Stevens
688 R Holyoake
689 Ronald Arthur Bentley
690 Mr & Mrs S Davis
691 Margaret Boiling
692 Mr & Mrs B McNeilly
693 David Parsons
694 Elaine Pickering
695 W Harper
696 Mrs G Sharman
697 Sam Adams
698 Alan Brock
699 Robert J Pegg
700 Dennis W Pegg
701 Lynda Bowmer
702 Albert Edward Hibbs
703 Mr & Mrs L Bowmer
704 Mr Ray Shreeve
705 J Nightingale
706 Donald A Watkinson
707 Joseph Thomas Fisher
708 Diana Elisabeth Stevenson
709 Margaret Joan Woodhouse
710 G D Riley
711 James Boal
712 John Smith
713 Lilian Calladine
714 Ian Stuart
715 T Bickerton
716 Marguerite W Thorn
717 Mrs June Harrison
718 Mr H Grimes
719 Mr B Averill

720 Mark Miley
721 Glynn Kearney
722 Thomas McColgan
723 M & D Webster
724 Mr & Mrs S P L Swift
725 W Gordon Lee
726 Philip Birks
727 Trevor B Tomlinson
728 Julia & Joe Sim
729 Mr P Johnson
730 Denise Lloyd
731 Neil Harrison
732 R E & K L Davis
733 Simon Gates Orgill
734 Mr J Fred Rushton
735 Mr & Mrs K A Birkin
736 Joan & Audrey Shaw
737 Kevin & Ena Burton
738 Albert Askey
739 Dean Francis Mottram
740 L D Hiles
741 John L Haskard
742 R A Sims
743 Roger John Illsley
744 Geoff Webb
745 J Hackman
746 E Towle
747 W J Lilley
748 Neil Patrick Smith
749 John J Hudson
750 Edward Billings
751 Emma Furnival
752 Raymond Barry Furnival
753 Tom Ryan
754 Keith Thomas
755 Mr & Mrs B Roulinson
756 Mr & Mrs G Whittaker
757 Mr J Salloway
758 A L Petitt
759 Mr & Mrs W Longdon
760 Mr & Mrs W Longdon
761 Graham Stendall White
762 Gary & Wendy Shapcott
763 Doris Miriam Shapcott
764 Duncan Chambers
765 David & Bev Lowe
766 Frank Morley
767 Ted & Beryl Olpin
768 Norman Holman
769 Mr John Hayes
770 Frank Rodgers
771 G N Davies (Australia)
772 Audrey Marshall
773 Keith Herbert & Sylvia Roe
774 Thomas Abel Howlett Earith
775 Miss A Fitt

776 K R Smith
777 Michael Pipes
778 Raymond Williamson
779 Mrs Jacqueline Horwer
780 Mrs K Biddle
781 Antony P Bray
782 Tony Alexander Myersclough
783 Florence Sellors
784 Mrs A M Parker
785 Dorothy Elizabeth Williams
786 Beavis S Alton
787 W T Atkins
788 Peter Capewell
789 Eric Buxton
790 Michael J Robotham
791 Kevin Flinn
792 Harold Fellows
793 June Gill
794 June Gill
795 June Gill
796 Wendy & Simon Lee
797 Ruth James
798 Mrs Lynne Stringer
799 Mrs Lynne Stringer
800 Pete Coxon
801 Mr & Mrs F Record
802 Arnold & Beryl Woodhouse
803 Anthony John Shaw
804 Norman Gregory Shaw
805 Margaret Hayward
806 Doris & Ian Whitney
807 Keith Kelly
808 B J Groves
809 Lawrence Woodings
810 Mrs V Thirkill
811 John R Blackwell
812 Eric E Linnett
813 V J O'Brien
814 L A Seale